PARSIFAL'S PAGE

KINGFISHER
An imprint of Kingfisher Publications Plc
New Penderel House, 283-288 High Holborn
London WC1V 7HZ
www.kingfisherpub.com

First published in the United Kingdom by Kingfisher 2005
2 4 6 8 10 9 7 5 3 1

A CIP catalogue record for this book
is available from the British Library.

ISBN-13: 978 0 7534 1008 0
ISBN-10: 0 7534 1008 7
Printed in India

1TR/0405/THOM/SGCH/90GSM/C

PARSIFAL'S PAGE

GERALD MORRIS

KINGFISHER

"'Open!'
'To whom? Who is there?'
'I wish to enter your heart.'
'Then you want too narrow a space.'
'How is that? Can't I just squeeze in? I promise not to jostle you. I want to tell you marvels.'"

Wolfram von Eschenbach, *Parzival*

CONTENTS

*This one is for William,
and also for Katherine Paterson* –

G.M.

1

THE SMITH'S BOY

Piers worked the bellows slowly and steadily, the way his father was always nagging him to do it. The forge was hot, and his new scarlet hat with the long yellow plumes, already damp from the sweat on his forehead, only made him hotter. Piers wanted to take the hat off, but he couldn't. His father had called the hat foppish and unsuitable for man's work, and Piers would have cut his own hand off before admitting that his gauche and uncultured father was right. Piers's mother had given him the hat just this morning. Perhaps it was true that the hat really was better suited to a castle than a smith's workshop, but then, Piers reflected disgustedly, so was he.

"Keep the bellows steady, Piers," his father said without looking up, giving all his attention to the long knife blade he was mending.

Piers, who had slowed while he mused on his father's boorishness, resumed his chore, replying only, "My name isn't Piers. It's Pierre."

Piers's father snorted but made no other answer until he had finished the knife blade. He plunged it into a bucket of water to cool, then examined it carefully. "Bah! And they call this steel," he muttered. "'Twill surely break again in a month." Laying the knife down on the bench, he looked at Piers critically. "'Twas well enough done, lad. Soon I should be teaching you the trade. We could start tomorrow, if you like. I've a batch of long nails to make. Rough work, nothing too hard. Should you like that?"

Piers made no effort to hide his revulsion, and his father's expression darkened. Before he could speak, though, Piers's mother swept into the shop. "La! Look at you, my Pierre! But you've soot all over your clothes! And your hands! *Mordieu!* Shall I ever get them clean?" With a flutter of skirts and a flash of petticoats, she whisked Piers away from the forge and back into the neat cottage across the yard. Piers couldn't resist casting a triumphant look over his shoulder at his glowering father.

While Piers watched his mother fuss over his smudged clothing, he wondered for the thousandth time what had possessed her, the beautiful Marie de Champagne, formerly a lady-in-waiting to a French noblewoman, to marry the rough and oafish blacksmith Giles. Piers could not doubt that they loved each other, for he could see how their faces softened when their eyes met, but all who knew them agreed that there was never a more mismatched pair. Marie was all energy and light and beauty, and she wore her homespun dresses with as much assurance as a great lady would wear a silken gown. Giles, for his part, was silent and brooding, a man of smouldering fires, heavy labour and unspoken thoughts. And yet, when they sat by the fire on winter evenings and smiled at each other, they were – in some way that Piers couldn't understand – one.

Only regarding their son did they ever quarrel. Giles wanted Piers to be a lowly smith like him, but Marie dreamed of the day when Piers, too, would know the great courts of Europe. She would tell him tales of the courts where she had lived, of the sumptuous fashions there, of the rules of courtship and chivalry among the knights and ladies. Piers remembered every word, every detail, and his dreams were full of brocade and tapestry and plumed helms shining in the sun.

But today, remembering his father's words about

learning to make nails, Piers felt those dreams slipping away. *"Maman,"* he said suddenly, "am I not old enough to be a squire?"

His mother smiled affectionately at him. "But no, *petit*. You are but eleven years old. Even the youngest squire must be at least thirteen. You could be no more than a page until then."

"Then can I be a page?" Piers demanded.

She shook her head sadly. "You would be a charming page, my pet. Especially in the new hat I made for you. But it is different here in Britain than in France. The English knights use few pages. It is regrettable, but what is to be done?" Indignant, Piers opened his mouth to complain about the cruel injustice of having been born English, when there came the sound of hoof-beats outside, and Piers's mother, looking out the window, exclaimed, *"Mordieu!* A knight!"

Crowding each other at the window, Piers and his mother watched as a knight rode a great sorrel stallion and led two other horses across the yard to the forge. He talked for several minutes with Piers's father, and then dismounted. Agog with curiosity and excitement, Piers slipped away from his mother and hurried across the yard to where the knight stood with the smith.

"Mind you mar it not," the knight said, handing

Piers's father his helm. "They told me in the village that you could do fine work, but I misdoubt it."

"'Twould be hard to mar this," Giles said, surveying the helm with evident disgust. "Have you no better armour, sir? For this is worthless."

The knight stared at Giles, his mouth open. "I beg your pardon?"

"Look," Giles said scornfully. "Fully six inches of leather strap showing here. One cut from a sword, and your helm is loose on your shoulders, bouncing off your ears every time you move."

The knight started to reply indignantly, but then saw what the smith was pointing at and understood. "It . . . I was told it was the very best."

"I make no doubt you were," Giles said. "Well, I'll mend it for you, though I waste my time."

The knight looked thoughtful. "Where could I get some other armour? Do you—" He looked sharply around the shop and then stopped as his eyes fell on a red suit of armour against the back wall. "That armour! Is it good?"

"Ay, it's fair enough armour," Giles admitted. "But too large for you. I know another who has armour, in Chester."

"I'll have no armour but that!" the knight declared grandly. "Never have I seen such beautiful arms."

"Huh," Giles said, curling his lips. "Yes, very pretty. I was going to do more work on it, though. That red suit belonged to a knight down in Cornwall, a nasty fellow called the Knight of the Red Lands. He was killed by Sir Gareth, of Arthur's court, and one of the Red Knight's servants sold me the armour for food. I've knocked out the dents and fixed the holes, but as I say, it's the wrong size. The Red Knight must have been a strapping big fellow, and you aren't."

"Then I must tighten the straps. That armour is perfect for my quest!"

Piers, watching from the door to the shop, gaped with awe at the knight. His mother's tales were filled with stories of quests. Giles only looked amused. "On a quest, are you, then?"

"No," the knight said, lifting his chin. "I am not on *a* quest. I am on *the* Quest."

Giles stood completely still. "*The* Quest?" he repeated slowly. "What do you mean?"

"I seek the highest prize of all. My quest is to save the land and restore the king."

Piers felt his breast swell with the majesty of the knight's calling, and even Giles seemed moved. In a soft voice, he said, "Do you mean King Arthur?"

The knight's lips curled scornfully. "No, I speak of a greater king than Arthur."

Piers's father stared at the knight, his eyes searching the knight's face hopefully, but before he could speak again, Piers rushed into the room. "Sir!" he cried. "On this quest, do you ... do you need a page?"

Giles frowned, but the knight only laughed. With one gauntleted hand, he reached out and touched Piers's new hat. "In sooth, thou lookst the part," he said. "And it is very true that I may be needing a page very soon. But you know it is not the fashion to have English boys as pages. It is the mode to have French pages or none at all."

"*Mais, c'est bon! Moi, je suis français. Vraiment! Ma mère est française,*" Piers exclaimed excitedly.

"Eh?"

"I said that I *am* French. My mother is a Frenchwoman. Will you take me with you? I know everything that a page does! My mother has taught me!"

"But ... your parents ..." the knight stammered.

"Pierre." It was his mother's voice, behind him at the door.

Piers whirled around. "Oh, mother, say I may! It is such a chance! You said that English knights do not use pages, but this one says he needs one. You can't say no!"

Marie looked across the shop at Giles, and Piers's

7

heart sank. His father would never permit it.

"You say that you are on *the* Quest," Giles said to the knight.

"I am."

Giles nodded, his face sober. "Then my son may go with you."

The next hour Piers spent in a daze of elation. He felt no sorrow, not even at leaving his mother, for he was already dreaming of the day when he would be a great courtier, perhaps in the service of King Arthur himself, and would come back to take his mother to the splendid castle where he lived. When all his things were packed, when his mother had used up her embarrassing tears, when the knight had been strapped into his new red armour, and when Piers was settled on one of the knight's spare horses, his father came from the smith's shop holding a long bundle.

"Sir knight, we should know your name," Giles said steadily.

"My name," said the knight, pausing dramatically, "is Ither Gahaviez, the nephew of King Uther Pendragon!"

Piers gawked at the knight, unable to comprehend his good fortune. Uther was King Arthur's father. Piers was the new page to the king's cousin. But his father only nodded absently.

"Then, Sir Ither, if you are truly on the Quest, you must have this." Unwrapping the bundle, he produced a long sword. The blade gleamed dully, and a few gems sparkled from the otherwise plain black haft.

"It is very kind of you," Sir Ither said politely. "But as you see, I have a sword." With a flourish, he drew his own sword and held it out for Giles to see. Giles looked at it without expression, and then, in a move almost too swift for Piers's eyes, he swung his own sword down on Sir Ither's blade. Giles's sword cut through the other blade as if it were a twig, and Sir Ither gaped at the half-blade he held in his hand.

"That will not happen with this sword, Sir Ither. It was forged over twenty years ago by a famous armourer from the land of the faeries. It was made for one reason: to be used on the Quest."

"I'll buy it!" Sir Ither said eagerly.

But Giles only shook his head impatiently. "No! If you buy it, it is worth nothing. Take it. It is a gift." The smith handed the sword to Sir Ither, then turned to Piers. "Go with God, my son," he said curtly, and then he turned his back and walked away.

Piers watched him go and felt only shame at his father's lies. When Giles had handed the blade to

Sir Ither, Piers had seen on the haft an ornate, writhing letter "T" – a mark that he had seen often on the old arms and armour in his father's shop. This blade was no faery sword. His father had been telling a silly children's story to make himself sound important.

Piers rode dutifully behind Sir Ither, waiting eagerly for his new master to speak again. From time to time, Sir Ither would utter a deep, meaningful sentence that Piers would immediately commit to memory. Once he said, "The sky is as fair as my lady love, than whom there is nothing so fair." Another time Sir Ither sighed and said, "Ah, my love! I could not love thee, dear, so much, loved I not honour more!" This saying sounded so grand that Piers almost wept. He hoped that someday he would be able to understand it.

Once Piers ventured to ask Sir Ither the identity of his lady love, but from the way that Sir Ither turned sharply in his saddle, his brows drawn, it was clear that Piers had committed some horrible trespass. "Hear me, boy! A page may speak when spoken to, and may deliver messages, but he must never ask impertinent questions! What you need to know, I will tell you!" Piers began to stammer an apology, but Sir Ither waved his hand graciously and continued, "Remember this lesson and never commit it again, but you are young, and I forgive you."

"Th-thank you, sir."

"I shall even answer your question. I have, alas, no lady love at this time, but rather I dream of the perfect lady whom I have yet to meet!"

Piers nodded sagely, pretending that he understood and trying to stifle his disappointment. Sir Ither's grand statements lost some of their lustre, being directed at a woman who existed only in his imagination. Piers realized he had much to learn about courtly love.

They made camp by a stream, and Piers hurried about, doing everything he could think of to make his master comfortable, and he was rewarded with a gracious word of approval that left him in transports. The next day, shortly before noon, Sir Ither stopped suddenly.

"Unless I be mistaken, boy, we are there!"

Piers started to ask where, but caught himself just in time.

Sir Ither smiled with satisfaction. "I had heard that he would be in this country. It is truly a good omen for the success of my quest that we should come to his camp so quickly. It is far better to meet him here than in his castle at Camelot!"

Piers felt almost faint. Camelot! The court of King Arthur himself! Did Sir Ither mean that they had come to a royal encampment? Through the trees ahead, Piers saw a meadow, and at the far side, several tents in a circle.

"There is Arthur's insignia! We are here!" Ither declared, and Piers had never felt so happy.

"Are you a knight?"

Piers almost fell from his horse at the strange voice that had spoken not three feet away. He had heard no other sound and seen no movement, but there at his side was a tall, amazingly muscular young man with shaggy hair and no beard. He wore ill-fitting homespun clothes and no shoes. Several hunting spears hung loosely from a strap over his shoulder. Sir Ither, who had also jumped in surprise, whirled about and glared at the man. "Begone, yokel!"

The young man cocked his head curiously. "What is a yokel?"

"You are!"

"Oh. Are you a knight?"

Sir Ither scowled. "As you see!" he snapped.

"I want to be a knight."

Sir Ither laughed harshly. "Well, you can't be. So go away."

"Is that armour?"

12

"Go away, knave, or feel my whip."

"Why is your armour red?"

With a muffled oath, Sir Ither snatched a riding whip from his saddle and flicked it at the young man's face. Piers did not see how it happened, but the young man moved ever so slightly, and the whip missed him. "I want to be a knight," the young man repeated placidly. "And I want red armour."

Angrily, jerking his head away from the young man, Sir Ither placed his helm on his head and booted his horse sharply. Eyes straight ahead, Piers followed his master into the meadow. A movement at his left, though, made him peek from the corners of his eyes. The youth was trotting easily beside them, faster than most men could run but showing no sign of exertion. Piers wished he would go away, before Sir Ither really hurt him.

They crossed the long meadow and approached the neat circle of tents. There was an enclosure for horses, empty now, and several wagons behind the tents. Piers saw many signs of knights – pennants and scattered arms and armour – but no knights until they were almost at the edge of the camp. Then a large man with a heavy black beard, grey at the corners of his mouth, stepped out of the largest tent and barred their way.

"Help you?" the large man said gruffly.

"I seek Arthur, who styles himself king!" Sir Ither said.

"I want to be a knight," said the young rustic.

The large man grinned mockingly. "I'm afraid you're both doomed to be disappointed. Arthur's not here, and he doesn't need any more knights."

The large man turned away, but Sir Ither rode his horse up to him. "Hold, my good man!"

"I'm not your good man," the large man said quietly.

"This is Arthur's camp, is it not?"

"It is. But Arthur's off hunting with a batch of clodpoles who, as you might say, style themselves knights."

"Who art thou, varlet?"

"My name's Kai."

Sir Ither caught his breath and looked sharply at the man. Piers did, too. He knew from his mother's stories about King Arthur's foster brother Kai, who had defeated two kings single-handedly in the Battle of the Five Kings, and who now served as seneschal for King Arthur. The rustic stepped between Piers and Sir Kai. "I do want to be a knight. And I need armour."

Sir Kai looked again at the young man, and this time his eyes showed a glint of interest. "Ay, my boy. That you do."

"I like red," the youth added earnestly.

Sir Ither spoke suddenly. "I shall wait for Arthur. Direct me to his tent."

"No," Sir Kai said. He looked coldly at Sir Ither and folded his arms.

Just then two women stepped out of the largest of the tents. Both were clad in gorgeous silk dresses, the sort that Piers's mother had described in such loving detail. The taller, and more beautiful, of the two spoke. "What is it, Kai?" She was holding a golden goblet, and had evidently been interrupted at her luncheon.

Sir Kai turned his head to speak to the lady, and Sir Ither took his heavy iron helm from its place on his saddle and brought it down with a solid thud on the back of Sir Kai's head. Sir Kai toppled forward immediately, and Piers gasped in horror. The tall lady froze with astonishment, but the other lady hurried to Sir Kai's prone form.

"What is thy name, my lady?" Sir Ither asked the tall lady politely, as if he had not just villainously struck down an unarmed man.

The lady's face was pale, and she looked unsteady, but she took a deep breath and stood straight. "My name is Guinevere. I do not ask for your name, for the names of recreant knights mean nothing to me."

"And yet I give it all the same, my lady," said Sir Ither, dismounting. "I am Ither, the nephew of King Uther Pendragon. I am rightful king over all England. I have been on quest these many months, seeking your misbegotten husband to challenge him to single combat. He is no true king of England!"

Piers's head was in a whirl. Everyone in England knew how the young Arthur, King Uther's only son, had been hidden away from the king's enemies by none other than Merlin the Enchanter, to be raised by the good knight Sir Ector. Everyone knew how Arthur had first proven his divine right to be king by drawing the great sword, Excalibur, from a stone and then had proven himself again and again through his wise rule. How could Sir Ither think that just being King Uther's nephew gave him the right to put all this aside? Indeed, Sir Ither had shown himself utterly unworthy of the throne, by striking down Sir Kai from behind.

The young rustic seemed to feel the same. Rising from the unconscious Sir Kai's side, he asked, "Are you sure that you are a knight? I met a knight one time, and he told me that knights fight fairly. I do not think that this was very knightly."

"That it was not," Queen Guinevere said, her voice shaking. "I see before me one man and one churl, and the churl wears the armour."

"Churl, am I?" Sir Ither snapped. Stepping forward, he snatched the golden goblet from the queen and abruptly threw the contents on her breast. A dark stain of red wine spread slowly down her gown. Sir Ither laughed and mounted his horse. "I'll be back, my lady, when you are a widow." Sir Ither turned his horse and rode back across the meadow. His heart heavy, Piers followed.

Sir Ither stopped in an open area beside a stream, less than a mile from the king's camp. "This will do nicely," he said. There was satisfaction on his face. "Boy, I want you to go back to Arthur's camp now. Show the king this cup and tell him that if he wants revenge, I will be waiting for him here. Tell him that none may come but the king himself, but I think he will come after the insult I've just given his wife." Piers could not speak, but his disgust for his master must have shown on his face, because Sir Ither added, "When I am king, I will speak to you about looking at me in that way, boy. Now go!"

The camp was very much astir when Piers arrived. Evidently the king had returned from the hunt. The horse enclosure was filled with lathered, panting horses. Beardless men in bright hunting clothes bustled everywhere. No one took any notice of Piers, and he was able to ride through the perimeter unchallenged. In the inner circle of the tents was a clump of people gawking at something, and as Piers drew near he saw to his relief that Sir Kai was sitting up in their midst, holding his head but clearly alive. The same woman who had knelt over him before was holding him up, and a man with a grey beard knelt beside him. As Piers approached they all looked up at him.

"That's the fellow's servant," Sir Kai said, blinking. "I recognize the silly hat."

The grey-bearded man stood. "Have you a message for me?"

Piers swallowed and said, "I have a message for King Arthur."

The man looked into Piers's eyes. "I am Arthur."

Piers burst into tears. From his cradle he had dreamed of the day when he might see this greatest of all men, and now that he finally saw him, he had to deliver a hateful message. King Arthur's eyes softened. "Come, boy. No one blames you for your master's incivility."

"Oh, incivility you call it," Sir Kai said with a snort.

"Be quiet, Sir Kai," said the woman beside him.

"There, I told you so," said another voice. It was the young rustic, appearing from nowhere, as he had in the forest. "I told you he wasn't acting very knightly."

Distracted, King Arthur looked at the youth. "And who are you, friend?"

"My name is Parsifal. I want to be a knight. I met a knight one time, about two years ago, or maybe more. It was in a different world. He told me that you could make me a knight. If you are really King Arthur. Are you?"

The king nodded gravely. "I am, friend. But this is not a good time."

"When would be a good time?"

King Arthur looked annoyed momentarily, but then replied patiently. "My friend, I cannot make anyone a knight who has not achieved great deeds. Knighthood must be earned."

"I shall do great deeds, then," the young man said happily.

The king turned back to Piers. "I beg your pardon, son. Tell me your message."

"My master, Sir Ither, is waiting for you in a small clearing to the east. He wants to fight you, your highness. No one else."

King Arthur pursed his lips, and Sir Kai struggled to his feet. "You can't go, Arthur," he said.

"Tell me why I can't, Kai," Arthur said. "I'll defeat him, you know."

"I know that, but you still can't go. The King of All England can't go off to meet every halfwit who challenges him. Send someone else."

"Who?" Arthur said. "You can't go with a cracked head. Gawain's in Orkney. I don't have any seasoned knights here. These are all journeymen, Kai."

"I'll go fight him," said the rustic, Parsifal.

"Will you shut up?" Kai snapped irritably. "Look, Arthur, this knight has no honour. Why should you respect his wishes? Send all the knights after him."

"I'll fight him by myself," Parsifal said. "I'm not afraid."

"Well, you ought to be, clodpole!" retorted Sir Kai. "He's a grown knight, and you're a puppy in bad clothes. He'd kill you."

Parsifal smiled. "I'm not the one he hit on the head," he said pleasantly.

The lady who had been helping Sir Kai burst into laughter, and Sir Kai whirled around, glaring. "Oh, you think that's funny, Lady Connoire?"

"Yes, actually," she said, still chuckling.

"You haven't so much as smiled since you came to court," Sir Kai said. "And now you think *this* is funny."

Lady Connoire lifted her chin. "Yes, especially

when I remember how you looked, face down in the mud."

"Why don't you go to the women's tent and be quiet?" Sir Kai said.

Lady Connoire stopped laughing. "Don't ever tell me to be quiet."

Sir Kai leaned close to her. "Be quiet," he said softly.

Immediately Lady Connoire slapped Sir Kai's cheek, and just as quickly Sir Kai slapped hers. Piers gasped, and Arthur snapped, "Kai!" but before he could move, Parsifal reached over and pulled Sir Kai away from Lady Connoire.

"My mother says that a knight should never show violence to a lady. You should not have done that."

Sir Kai's face was a deep red, but he scowled at Parsifal and said, "Go away, ploughboy. Just go away!"

Parsifal nodded patiently. "I will, but I ought to have some armour, so I can do my great deeds. Do you have any red armour? I like red."

"I'll give you some red armour," Sir Kai said furiously. "It's on that idiot knight back in the woods!" With a jerk, Sir Kai turned and stormed away.

"Oh, can I have his? That will be fine," Parsifal

said, and he too turned and began running across the meadow.

"I beg pardon on behalf of my brother," King Arthur said gently to Lady Connoire.

"Do not trouble yourself, sire," said Lady Connoire stiffly, and then she too strode away, leaving King Arthur with Piers in the midst of a shocked circle of onlookers.

"I don't believe I've ever felt so left out of a conversation," the king said quietly, his lips curling slightly. "My boy, I fear we've been discourteous. Please tell your master that I decline his challenge on the grounds that I find him boorish and unworthy of my time." Piers nodded, but hesitated.

"Is there something else?" the king asked.

"Yes, your highness." Piers reached into his saddlebag and took out the golden cup that Sir Ither had stolen from Queen Guinevere. "Please, sire, give this back to the queen."

King Arthur nodded, his eyes filled with understanding. "I thank you, son," he said. "If you should ever happen to have a change of master, I would be very happy to see you again. Now, you'd best go before this Parsifal gets himself in trouble."

Piers nodded and turned his horse. Parsifal was already across the meadow and into the woods.

Piers urged his horse on, but he didn't catch up until he came to Sir Ither's clearing. There was Parsifal, holding Sir Ither's body by his ankles and dragging it around in a circle. One of Parsifal's short spears protruded from the visor of Sir Ither's helm. Parsifal looked up as Piers entered the clearing. "How do you get this stuff off?" he asked.

2

PARSIFAL'S EDUCATION

It took Piers and Parsifal over an hour to remove Sir Ither's armour and buckle it securely onto Parsifal, whom it fit perfectly. Parsifal walked slowly around the clearing.

"It is very fine," he said gravely. "But it will be difficult to run."

"But knights do not run," Piers said. "They ride horses."

"I do not know how to ride a horse," Parsifal said thoughtfully. "I shall have to learn." He walked around the clearing again, then tried to take off his helm. After a moment, Piers helped him.

"See, here is the strap to pull."

Parsifal took off the helm and took a deep breath. "That's better. I couldn't see, and the sounds were all wrong inside there. Must I wear this hat often?"

"It's called a helm," Piers explained. "And you only need wear it when you fight."

"That's good." Parsifal moved his arms stiffly. "How shall I fight, though? I cannot draw my arms back far enough to throw my javelin well."

Piers had been hoping for this opening. "Oh, sir, you mustn't fight with a javelin! It is common and rude and not knightly."

"Knights do not use javelins?" Piers shook his head, and Parsifal said, "But this fellow had a spear, too."

"That's not a spear; it's a lance. Knights hold their lances against their bodies and ride their horses toward their enemies and hit them with the points of the lances."

Parsifal's eyes widened. "That is what knights do?" Piers nodded again, and Parsifal looked earnestly at the page. "Tell me truly. Are knights not very clever?"

"Oh, sir! Do not say that! Knights are the noblest and finest of all men!" Parsifal shook his head thoughtfully. "Indeed they are!" Piers protested. "You will see when you are used to it. The lance is the very prince of weapons. And a fine sword is nearly as grand."

Parsifal's brow cleared. "Yes, of course. The sword." He withdrew from the scabbard the sword that Piers's father had given Sir Ither. "Yes, this is good. Such a weapon makes me feel strong." He waved the sword in the air, clearly still struggling against the confines of his armour. He turned to Piers. "Knights do not wear their armour all the time. How do they take it off at night?"

"The same way they put it on," Piers replied.

"But I cannot do that without you. And how will I put it back on in the morning?"

Piers hesitated, then said, "I could ride with you, if you like. My former master is dead, and I did not wish to serve such a man anyway."

"Oh, that will be all right, then," said Parsifal, smiling happily. "I like you."

Piers liked Parsifal too, but he could not help thinking how far his star had fallen in just one day. This morning he was page to a royal prince, a nephew of the late king, Uther Pendragon, and now he was a page to an unknown rustic with great strength and grand dreams but nothing else to recommend him. Still, it's better than being a blacksmith, he reminded himself.

"What is your name?" Parsifal asked.

"Pierre," Piers said. "It is French."

"Oh, are you French?"

"Yes," Piers said. It was half true, anyway.

"Is that why you wear a funny hat?"

26

Piers started to reply angrily, but stopped himself. Just because his new master was ignorant did not mean he could behave discourteously himself. He would have to show Parsifal how knights behave by example. "It is *un chapeau d'un courtisan*," he said grandly.

"Is that French for 'funny hat'?" Parsifal asked.

Piers sighed. "Something like that," he said resignedly.

"Pierre?" asked Parsifal, a crease on his forehead.

"Yes, Sir Parsifal?"

"'Sir'? Why do you call me 'Sir'?" Parsifal asked curiously.

"It is how one speaks of knights."

"But I am not a knight until I have done great deeds. The king said so."

Piers realized that he was unsure of the protocol here. Parsifal was right. "What should I call you then?"

"Parsifal. It is my name."

Piers felt sure that a page did not call his master by his given name, but he could think of no other option here. He resolved privately never to use the name unless they were alone. "Very well... er... Parsifal. Did you have a question for me?"

"Oh, yes. I was just wondering what I do with the armour when I have to make water. Must I take it all off?"

Piers cringed at the indelicacy of the question, but in fairness he admitted that it was something Parsifal should know. For the next few minutes they explored the various hinges and openings in the armour that enabled a knight to relieve himself with relative convenience. Parsifal found these fascinating, and Piers could only hope that the novelty would wear off and his new master would soon stop playing with his armour.

Piers rode in his pagely position behind Parsifal and watched his master try to stay in the saddle. It was not a pretty sight, but even in the course of one afternoon, Piers could see improvement. Although the depths of Parsifal's ignorance continued to amaze Piers, Parsifal was also an astonishingly quick learner, and he never forgot anything. It had been awkward getting Parsifal into the saddle for the first time, but when he promptly fell off the other side, it had been much easier to get him up again. By the time that Parsifal had learned how to stay on his horse, he was able to climb into the saddle unassisted. Piers knew from his mother's stories that some knights never did learn to mount their horses while in armour and always required some assistance. While there were surely gaps in Parsifal's knowledge, Piers could discern no limits to his physical strength and coordination.

Piers smelled woodsmoke, and then a moment later saw a peasant's cottage over the heath where they were riding. He sighed with resignation, and sure enough, as they drew near to the cottage, Parsifal slowed his horse and bowed his head politely to the gawking yokels outside the little hut. "How do you do?" Parsifal said. "I hope that you are well today."

The peasants did not answer, but Parsifal did not seem to mind. He touched his horse with his heel and cantered away again.

Piers rode by the hovel, eyes straight ahead. There did not seem to be anything he could do to squelch Parsifal's incurable desire to greet every person whom he encountered, but he did not have to join him in his plebeian habits. The first time that it had happened – Parsifal had stopped to greet a greasy pork-butcher on his way home from market – Piers had suggested that it was not very knightly to say hello to every person, of every station in life. But Parsifal had only said, "Before I left home, my mother told me to greet all I met."

"Perhaps she meant for you to greet all other

knights," Piers said.

"She did not say so. I will do what my mother said." Parsifal's voice was pleasant – indeed, it had never been anything but pleasant – but Piers heard the finality of his decision.

On the other hand, Piers had won the dispute over where he was to ride. When they had at last set off, Piers had fallen into position behind his master. Parsifal had complained that he wanted Piers to ride beside him, but Piers had been adamant. No page should ride alongside his knight. It was not seemly. At last Parsifal had conceded the point, perhaps because his mother had not told him any different.

About a mile after the peasant's cottage, they came upon a long tent made of what seemed to be silk. As they drew near, Piers could see a table set with a large dinner, and a beautiful woman seated at one end of the table. She was alone, and Piers's heart began to race. This looked like the beginning of an adventure, if his mother's stories were anything to go by.

Parsifal stopped and dismounted awkwardly. "How do you do?" he said. "I hope you are well today." The lady started to reply, but Parsifal did not wait for her. "I am hungry," he said.

Piers then watched with astonishment as Parsifal

strode to the table and picked up a whole roast chicken and began gnawing on it. "Sir!" Piers cried out, dismounting at once. "You mustn't—" Then he caught himself. A page should never reprove his master, especially in front of a lady.

As for the lady, she had risen to her feet, one hand over her breast, her face showing equal parts of astonishment and fear. Piers wanted to reassure her that she was in no danger, but a page should be quiet in his master's presence, and he had to content himself with smiling reassuringly at her. She did not seem reassured.

"I beg you, sir knight, do not hurt me," the lady said faintly.

"Oh, I won't hurt you. Do you have anything to drink?" Parsifal said. At least that was probably what he said. It was hard to make out his exact words since he was speaking through huge mouthfuls of chicken. In less than a minute, the chicken was gone, and the bones were scattered carelessly about the table, leaving greasy spots on the pure white tablecloth. Parsifal reached for a flagon of liquid and began drinking right from the jug.

"What is this?" he declared. "It tastes funny."

"It's . . . wine," the lady whispered.

"Is that what wine tastes like? Bleah!" Parsifal cleared his throat and spat noisily onto the table.

"Haven't you any water, ma'am?" She shook her head, and Parsifal shrugged. "It's just as well, I suppose. The more I drink, the more I have to make water, and it's not so easy in armour, even though I have this little door here." Parsifal pointed at his little door, and the lady nodded rigidly, her eyes wide. Piers longed for a hole to open up in the ground for him to crawl into.

Parsifal started on a leg of lamb and gestured to Piers. "Come on, Pierre. Tuck in. There's plenty. You, too, ma'am." Piers shook his head and tried to communicate an abject apology to the lady with his eyes, but she did not look his way. She only stared at Parsifal in unblinking amazement. After Parsifal finished the leg of lamb, he leaned back and erupted with a loud belch. "There," he said happily. "That's better."

At this point the lady evidently felt that she should occupy Parsifal with conversation. "Have you . . . have you come far, sir knight?"

"I'm not a real knight yet. I have to do great deeds first," Parsifal confided to the lady. "No, we haven't come far. But I *was* getting peckish. Good thing you were here with all this food. Lucky. Do you do this often?"

"Do what?"

"Sit out here alone with a table full of food."

"I . . . am awaiting my husband, Duke Orilus," the lady said. "It is his birthday, and this was to be a surprise for him."

Parsifal stood and stretched. "Well, it will still be a surprise for him, won't it?" He moved his hands over his armour a moment, then laughed. "The worst thing about armour is that it's hard to scratch your itches." He smiled at the lady. "Aren't you glad that you can scratch whenever you like?"

The lady smiled weakly and said, "If you say, sir."

"Well, Pierre and I must be off to do great deeds," Parsifal said. "I'll just kiss you now."

"What?" gasped the lady and Piers in unison.

"My mother said that when I met a fair lady I should give her a kiss." He stepped quickly forward, took the lady's arms in his two hands and lifted her off the ground. She struggled weakly, but Parsifal did not seem to notice, and he kissed her on her cheek and set her down. Then he looked closely at her hand. "My mother also said I should take a ring from the fair lady I kissed," he said, and before either could say another word, he took a jewelled ring from the lady's hand. Then he walked back to his horse, dropped the ring in his saddlebag, and mounted. "Come along, Pierre," he said, smiling. "I'd like to do at least one great deed before dark."

Clearly Piers had a formidable task before him, if he was ever to make Parsifal a true knight. He began that evening, as they sat around a campfire eating a roast boar that Parsifal had killed with one of his javelins shortly after they made camp.

"Parsifal?"

"Yes, Pierre," Parsifal said around a mouthful of food.

"I need to talk to you about what happened back at that lady's tent."

"Did something happen? I saw nothing."

Piers cleared his throat. "It is only that your behaviour there was not completely knightly."

Parsifal belched loudly. "In what way?" he asked.

"Well, there's a good example right there," Piers said, making the most of the moment. "Belching. Knights are not supposed to belch in front of ladies."

Parsifal frowned. "But sometimes I need to belch," he said.

"You must do it quietly when you are among ladies," Piers said.

"Why?"

"Because ladies don't belch, and we must respect their custom," Piers said firmly.

"Ladies don't belch?"

"No, they don't."

Parsifal pondered this for a moment, then said, "Sometimes when I have wind, I don't belch but instead I—"

"And they don't do that either!" Piers said hastily.

Parsifal shook his head with wonder. "Truly, ladies are amazing creatures. My mother should have told me."

"Yes, that's another thing. What exactly is it that your mother told you before you went out?"

Parsifal smiled. "She gave me much advice. She used to be a lady in a castle herself, you know – the Lady Herzeloyde – and so she knew about knights and things. She said that I should be good and kind and should greet everyone I meet – but you already knew that."

"Yes," Piers muttered.

"She said I should always be good to ladies and never show them violence."

"She said that? Then why did you handle the lady in the tent so roughly?"

"Was I rough?" Parsifal looked concerned. "I meant no harm. I just picked her up to kiss her better."

"But why did you kiss her at all?"

"Didn't you hear me tell the lady? My mother said that one day I would meet a lady who seemed to me to be fair above all others and that she would make me exceeding glad and that when we had kissed then I should give her a ring and she should give me one, and then we would be happy. I did not have a ring to give her, but she had one for me, so it was all right, was it not?"

Piers understood now. "I think she was talking about the woman you would marry," he said patiently.

"Marry? What is that?"

For a moment Piers could not speak. "You don't know what it means to marry? But your mother . . . where is your father?"

"I never knew my father," Parsifal said. "He rode off to a faraway place called Damascus when I was a baby, and he got killed. My mother was very sad, so she moved to our home in the woods."

Piers said, "To marry is when a man and a woman decide to love each other all the rest of their lives as they will never love anyone else."

Parsifal nodded slowly. "So you think she did not mean for me to kiss every fair woman?"

"That's right. You must never kiss any woman against her will, and you should never kiss any woman who is married to another man."

Parsifal nodded thoughtfully. "So I should not have taken her ring either?"

"No, you should not have!" Piers said emphatically. "Rings are exchanged only when two people get married."

"There are many rules for knights," Parsifal said ruefully. "And how will I know which lady I am to marry?"

This was the opening that Piers wanted. For the next two hours he told Parsifal everything he could think of about how men attract ladies, placing a heavy emphasis on polite conversation and table manners. As he wound up his discourse, he spent a few minutes describing courtly fashions for men, as his mother had described them, and ventured a hint that Parsifal's rough homespun clothes might be exchanged for others.

Parsifal frowned. "My mother made these clothes," he said, and Piers abandoned that subject. The personality of this Lady Herzeloyde was still stamped strongly on her son. There would be time later for such matters.

The next day, Piers and Parsifal came to a castle. It was not a large castle, but the pennants and escutcheons that hung from the battlements proclaimed it to be the residence of a knight and lord.

Parsifal turned in his saddle. "Is this a great deed?" he asked.

"Perhaps," Piers replied. "Knock at the gate and see what adventure awaits."

Parsifal banged on the heavy wooden gate, and a few minutes later it was opened by a manservant in stunning green and gold livery. Even in Arthur's camp, Piers had not seen such splendid male raiment. He wished he had an outfit like that and was glad that he at least had his new hat.

"How do you do?" Parsifal said. "I hope you are well today."

Piers winced. He hadn't thought to tell Parsifal the proper form to use when announcing your arrival. Of course usually a squire did the actual announcing, but pressing a point, Piers decided that with no squire at hand it would be all right for a page.

"Tell the lord of this manor," Piers proclaimed loudly, "that Sir... that Parsifal, lately of King Arthur's court, has arrived and seeks shelter."

Piers had barely finished speaking before an elderly man and a young lady came running from the central keep. Both were even more sumptuously dressed than the manservant. Piers wished his mother could see their clothes. "Sir Parsifal! Come in!" said the elderly man. "You are welcome in my castle, as is any knight of King Arthur's Round Table. I am Sir Gurnemains, and this is my daughter, the Lady Liase. I beg you to make as long a stay with us as you like."

Parsifal looked puzzled. "What is this round table?" he asked.

Piers cringed again. He did wish that Parsifal would stop betraying his ignorance through his habit of asking every question that came into his head.

"But did you not say...? Then where are you from?"

"I've come over from the Other Side," Parsifal said. He waved his arm back at Piers. "This is the one who shouted. Ask him what he meant."

Sir Gurnemains and Lady Liase looked at Piers, who said, "I apologize for being unclear. Sir... I mean, er... Parsifal is not yet a knight, but he has been sent out by King Arthur to do great deeds and to earn knighthood." He was afraid that Sir Gurnemains would be angry at having been led into a mistake, but Sir Gurnemains beamed.

"Nothing could be better!" he said. "For I, Sir Gurnemains, am an instructor of knights!"

Piers and Parsifal stayed at Sir Gurnemains's castle for three months, while Parsifal learned chivalry. Sir Gurnemains, although now retired, had once been mentor to some of King Arthur's most famous knights, including Sir Bagdemagus and Sir Griflet, and his knowledge of court customs was immense.

Parsifal was a willing pupil, once the issue of his clothing had been resolved. As soon as Sir Gurnemains saw Parsifal out of his armour, he had exclaimed, "But you are perfect! I've not seen such arms and shoulders since Sir Lancelot left the court! But my dear Sir Parsifal! That . . . that rag you are wearing! Really, it will not do!"

Parsifal's eyes never lost their amiable expression, but his lips set in what Piers had already recognized as a sign of inflexibility. Fearing that Parsifal would say something offensive, Piers hastily intervened. "Excuse me, Sir Gurnemains. Forgive my speaking out of turn, but that garment was a gift from . . . from my master's mother."

Sir Gurnemains recovered quickly. He bowed at once, with rare grace, and said, "I beg your pardon, Sir Parsifal. I did not know, or I should not have spoken. But, forgive me one question, do you do well to wear such a precious garment with your armour? Nothing will wear out a doublet faster than armour. Should you not wrap it in oilcloth to keep it forever? I can have some brought to you."

Piers gazed at Sir Gurnemains with admiration. Parsifal cocked his head and thought for a moment. Then he nodded. "You are right. But I have no other clothes."

"Oh, my dear boy, please allow me the honour of dressing you in a few of my own discarded clothes. They would only be thrown away, so it is no great loss. Please say yes."

"Thank you," Parsifal said simply.

And so it was that Sir Gurnemains proudly gave Parsifal three brilliant orange and green suits at breakfast the next morning. Having spent the night in the servants' hall, Piers knew that these "discarded" clothes had been sewn the night before by three ladies-in-waiting, but he said nothing.

"Come, Sir Parsifal," said Sir Gurnemains, when Parsifal had dressed. "We have much to do. We shall begin by learning how to bow. It is not so easy as you might think."

And so they began. Parsifal learned how to bow in all the different degrees, how to walk in a courtly fashion, and how to dance. The first few days were tense. It wasn't that Parsifal had difficulty. His natural grace made every physical exercise relatively easy for him. The problem was his inquisitive nature. Why should you bow differently to a queen than to a lady's maid? Why must knights prance like cats when they walk? Why do people dance? Piers, remembering when Parsifal asked the lady in the tent about scratching itches and seeking to avoid future embarrassments, ventured to mention the matter to Sir Gurnemains.

"Yes, he does ask a great many questions, doesn't he?" Sir Gurnemains said thoughtfully. "This always puts one in danger of impertinence. I shall speak to him." Piers bowed and began to back away, but Sir Gurnemains stopped him. "I have been meaning to speak to you anyway, my boy. What is your name?"

"Pierre," Piers said.

Sir Gurnemains looked pleased. "French, of course. How charming! I am so pleased that Sir Parsifal has a page such as you with him. For, you may have noticed, Sir Parsifal still has, shall we say, a few rough edges. If, like so many knights these days, he rode only with some boorish squire who cared for nothing but weapons, he would never get the sort of polish that, between us, we shall give him."

Piers flushed and bowed again.

Thus it was that from that time on, every

question that Parsifal asked received a gentle reproof from Sir Gurnemains and a reminder that there was no sin so horrible as the uncivil question. Parsifal never seemed completely to accept this dictum, though, and he had only moderate success. Although he was normally compliant, this rule irked Parsifal more than any other.

At last, though, after three months of intensive training in all the knightly courtesies, Parsifal had achieved some control over his curiosity and appeared to Piers to be a perfect knight. His bow was exquisite, and he could mince as daintily as a courtier of half his weight. But Piers was most proud on the final evening of Sir Gurnemains's course of instruction, when he watched his master, strikingly clad in green and orange, dancing faultlessly with the Lady Liase. No one would have recognized the rustic hunting boy in that gallant figure, tripping effortlessly around the ballroom.

"*Mon enfant,*" Sir Gurnemains cried as the dance came to an end, "you are complete to a shade! Never have I seen such grace on the dance floor! Why, not even Sir Lancelot could have surpassed you! And now, the final lesson: the kiss!"

Parsifal frowned and began to speak but caught himself.

"Ah, you want to know how I shall teach you the

courtly manner of the kiss!" Sir Gurnemains said, smiling at Parsifal and Liase. "Nothing is easier. You shall kiss my daughter Liase, for never have I known a knight more worthy—"

"I am not a knight, and I do not wish to kiss Liase," Parsifal said abruptly. "Please let us skip this lesson and go on."

For once, Sir Gurnemains was caught off guard and had no smooth response, and Liase looked stricken. Piers closed his eyes in anguish.

Parsifal continued. "If we are finished with bowing and using table manners and prancing and wearing pretty clothes, then I am glad. Now, if I may ask you—"

"Remember about asking questions," Sir Gurnemains said.

"I do not see how I am to learn anything unless I do," Parsifal replied.

"Why, you have already learned everything!" Sir Gurnemains said triumphantly. "I have nothing left to teach you."

Parsifal frowned. "You have not taught me how to use my sword or how to ride with a lance. You have not taught me how to achieve great deeds. All you have taught me is how to act like a knight, when I wanted to learn how to become one." He shook his head slowly. "I shall leave you tomorrow."

And so the next morning, while both Sir Gurnemains and his daughter wept at the gate, Piers and Parsifal rode away from the silver and polished crystal of Sir Gurnemains's castle, back into the forest.

3

JEAN LE FORESTIER

Piers and Parsifal rode due west for almost twelve hours, into the darkest forest Piers had ever seen. Both of their horses were staggering when at last Parsifal stopped near a tiny brook. "We shall camp here." Piers almost fell from the saddle and began stiffly to set about their camp needs, but Parsifal, after watching him for a moment, said, "Let me do that."

"But it isn't seemly for a knight to do his own labours," Piers protested weakly.

"You are doing my labours so poorly that I shall have to do them all again anyway. Here, help me undress, and I'll show you."

When Parsifal was free of his armour, he set about teaching Piers how to make camp in the woods. In no time, they were very comfortably settled, and Parsifal had disappeared soundlessly into the forest with one of his hunting spears, his face shining with anticipation. They ate well that night on the fruits of his hunt.

The next day they met the first human they had seen since leaving Sir Gurnemains, a freckle-faced young man in bright new armour. "How do you do?" Parsifal said politely. "I hope you are well today."

"Why, I'm middling, just middling," the youth said, eyeing Parsifal's armour with respect. "I say, are you someone I ought to know?"

"I don't know," Parsifal said, puzzled. "Who are you supposed to know?"

"I mean, are you someone famous? Like Sir Gareth or Sir Tristram or someone like that?" Parsifal shook his head, and the youth hastily apologized. "Oh, I'm sorry. It's just that you looked so, well, so deuced knightly, I thought you must be a great knight." Piers smiled proudly. Parsifal *did* look impressive. Sir Gurnemains had seen to it that the red armour had been shined and decked with any number of bright strips of silk.

"I do want to be a great knight," Parsifal said simply.

"So do I," the youth said enthusiastically. "I say, I don't suppose you'd want to try a pass at me in joust, would you? I daresay I'll get a fall from it, but it will be good practice."

"I would like it above all things," Parsifal said earnestly. "Tell me how to go about it."

"Oh, I can see you're roasting me," the youth said, laughing. "You're obviously far more experienced than I am. Shall we use this bare patch alongside the path? I'll start from that end."

The youth turned his horse and trotted away, and Piers realized for the first time that in all their months with Sir Gurnemains Parsifal had never so much as touched a lance. Indeed, he wouldn't even have one had Sir Gurnemains not put one on Parsifal's saddle as a convenient place to attach flags and guidons. Parsifal watched the youth closely, then imitated his every move on the other side of the bare patch.

It was over in a second. The two rode toward each other, and the nameless youth popped Parsifal very neatly from his horse. Parsifal landed with a crash, then sat up. "So that's how it's done," he said softly.

"I'm terribly sorry!" the youth cried, leaping from his horse. "Are you all right?"

"Yes, thank you," Parsifal said. "You did that very well. May I ask, are you known as a good jouster?"

The young man hesitated, but then he answered. "No, sir. I'm the worst jouster in the county. I must have just been lucky."

"I shall have to practise," Parsifal said thoughtfully. "It is more difficult than I would have thought." He stood and held out his hand to the youth. "Thank you very much for your lesson."

The youth shook Parsifal's hand and then, with wonder on his face, watched as Piers and Parsifal rode away. Piers felt a vague uneasiness. It was true that Parsifal looked splendid in his refurbished armour and new trappings, but he had not looked so very fine on his back in the dust. To avoid future embarrassments, Parsifal would just have to stay away from jousting, he concluded.

They continued west, toward Cornwall, passing through a few settled lands, but where he could, Parsifal always seemed to choose paths that led into the darkest, most forbidding, forests. On the third day, riding through dense shrubbery, they pushed through a thicket and came into a small clearing where an unkempt man was working with an axe. As soon as they were in sight, the woodcutter stopped his work and looked at them suspiciously.

"How do you do?" Parsifal asked, inclining his

49

head in a polite bow that Piers thought was probably not necessary when greeting a dirty peasant like this. "I hope you are well today."

The woodcutter's severe expression lightened, and he replied, "I am quite well, I thank you. And I return your good wishes." Piers was startled at the man's cultured speech, which even had a trace of a French accent.

"I am looking for great deeds to do," Parsifal said, trotting closer. "But I have not found any at all."

"I am afraid that all the great deeds in these environs were done last year. I am so sorry to disappoint you." The woodcutter's voice had a touch of amusement in it.

"It is very frustrating," Parsifal commented. "King Arthur said I had to do great deeds, but he did not say where to find them."

"King Arthur sent you to do great deeds?" the woodcutter asked. "It was not kind of him."

"Why not?" Parsifal asked. Then, glancing guiltily at Piers, he added, "If it is not impertinent of me to ask a question."

"No, my friend, but it might be impertinent of me to answer," the woodcutter said softly. "I wish you well." He turned back to his wood-chopping. Parsifal did not move. Watching his face, Piers could tell that he dearly wanted to ask the woodcutter what he meant, but was afraid to ask any more questions. At last the man looked up from his work. "Is there something else?" he asked.

Parsifal chose his words with care. "I do not mind if you are impertinent, if you would like to explain what you meant." Parsifal glanced defiantly at Piers. "It was not a question," he added.

The woodcutter shrugged. "I only meant that I have never seen a knight who seemed to me less likely to achieve great deeds. Except possibly Griflet," he added as an afterthought. "You hold your lance wrong. You're wearing your sword on the wrong side and too high to reach easily. Any decent fighter could take your weapons away from you in a trice."

Piers felt a deep indignation growing inside. It was bad enough to be unhorsed by a young knight, but it was worse to be laughed at by a yokel. "You forget your place, my man," Piers said to the woodcutter in a tight voice.

"As you say," the woodcutter replied. "Again, I wish you well."

Again, Parsifal did not move. "Could you take my weapons away from me?" he asked the woodcutter. The yokel paused, then nodded. "Show me," Parsifal said, dismounting.

The man shrugged. "Very well. Draw your sword and attack me."

"But I do not wish to hurt you. The sword is very sharp."

The woodcutter laughed. "You won't hurt me," he said.

Parsifal drew his sword, with some difficulty, and swung it at the man. He missed. One moment the man was there; the next he had slipped easily away.

"Try again."

Parsifal tried again. This time the woodcutter deflected the sword with a careless motion of his axe, reached inside Parsifal's guard, and flipped his visor down. Parsifal laughed and said, "How did you do that?"

The man only smiled. The next time Parsifal attacked, his sword buried itself in the dirt at the man's feet, and the woodcutter reached in and plucked off one of the silk banners that Sir Gurnemains had tied so carefully to Parsifal's armour. Then he took another. In five minutes, every cloth token had been ripped away and lay in the dust. Parsifal had not come even close to touching the woodcutter. Finally, with a lightning twist inside one of Parsifal's ponderous swings, a sharp blow from the blunt side of the axe on

Parsifal's fingers, the woodcutter plucked Parsifal's sword from his grasp.

"There," he said softly. "It was not so—" The woodcutter stopped abruptly, feeling the sword. "*Mordieu*," he whispered. He flashed right and left with the sword, and Piers thought for a frantic moment that the woodcutter was going to kill them both, but then the man lowered the point. "Never have I held such a blade. It is *merveilleux!* With such a blade, I could…"

Holding his numbed hand, Parsifal watched the woodcutter's rapt features. "Will you teach me to use it well, sir?" Parsifal asked meekly.

The woodcutter hesitated. "It will take one such as you a long time to learn," he said. "How can I do that? I have my labour."

"I will help you cut your wood in the morning. Together we can finish quickly. Then you can teach me. Please, sir."

Aghast but helpless, Piers watched the scruffy yokel consider Parsifal's surprising request. To Piers's dismay, the woodcutter nodded. "For the sake of this sword, I will teach you."

Parsifal grinned widely. "Thank you, sir. My name is Parsifal."

"I am Jean le Forestier. We rise an hour before dawn."

*

At dawn the next day, Piers was riding toward the nearest village, where there was a blacksmith. The woodcutter had given Piers a few copper coins and had instructed him to buy an axe. Jean le Forestier was already at work, and Parsifal had gone hunting. Piers had lain awake for what seemed hours the night before, wondering how long they would have to stay in this wretched hovel, and now he was sleepy and surly.

A full hour later, he came to the village where Jean had directed him. It took him no time to locate the blacksmith's shop, but when he looked at it, he wrinkled his nose in disgust. His father's shop had been so much more efficient. He told the sooty smith what he needed, and the man brought out a shiny axe with a new handle. Piers glanced at it carelessly and started to pay, but then stopped. "What's this?" he asked. He looked more closely at the blade. "Here, man, what sort of chicanery is this? Do you call this steel?"

The smith gaped at him, but immediately launched into a whining protest. "But, young master, it is the very best I have! Do you see that shine?"

"Ay," Piers said with a sniff. "And I see that flaw there, too. This has been mended, and by someone who didn't know his business either. 'Twould break after two blows, I daresay."

The smith scowled, but he did not argue. Instead he went back inside and brought out another axe. This was not so shiny as the first, but when Piers examined it carefully, desperately trying to recall everything his father had ever said about blades and axes, he found no defects. "Right, then. 'Twill do. Sharpen it, and I'll be off."

"But, young master, it could not be any sharper! Look at that edge!"

Piers laughed. The one skill that his father had ever truly complimented him on was his touch with a whetstone. "Show me your stone, man," Piers said. He dismounted and took the axe inside. It was a poor whetstone, but Piers could make do. Minutes later he held up the axe for the smith's examination. "Now, my man, try to be more honest in thy dealings or my master'll come back and shave thy bottom with this edge."

The smith reverently ran his finger along the blade and nodded. Piers paid for the axe and left, feeling an odd sense of accomplishment.

Thus began another three months of training, months that were as tedious to Piers as the months at Sir Gurnemains's had been to Parsifal. Every morning the two men took their axes to the woods and worked side by side until noon. Then, after a luncheon, Jean would begin Parsifal's training. At first they worked on swordplay, using stout wooden cudgels. Jean showed Parsifal the most basic moves and drilled him incessantly on these, but when the shadows grew long and it came near time to stop, Jean le Forestier would show Parsifal some more elaborate tricks.

Considering the matter, Piers decided that this rough woodsman must have been squire to a great knight at one time. It was sad to think of someone falling so far in station, but it must surely have been Jean's fault. Probably he had been turned off for some crime or even for being too coarse. Perhaps Jean's master had demanded that Jean shave once in a while, Piers reflected.

As a matter of pride, Piers saw to it that even in this desolate and lonely clearing his master always had the appearance of a knight. He shaved Parsifal often and trimmed his hair at least once a week. He even offered to give the woodcutter a shave once, but to his relief Jean rejected the suggestion. Except for these few personal tasks and for occasionally sharpening the men's axes with Jean's small hand-held whetstone, Piers had little to do and was usually bored.

After a month of working with cudgels, Jean le Forestier disappeared into the forest one afternoon and returned with a sword, still crusted with clay from having been buried, and a shield. It was just as Piers had thought. The man had been a squire but he had stolen his master's arms and had had to flee. Now Jean and Parsifal sparred with real swords, and although Piers had little interest in swordplay and did not watch closely, it soon became clear to him that Parsifal was as quick a learner as ever. Even Jean began to bestow some grudging praise on Parsifal. "You may someday deserve that sword of yours yet," he said gruffly one evening. "Tomorrow we shall work on jousting."

Piers began taking walks in the woods during the long afternoons of weaponry. He had never spent much time in the forests near his home, but now he found that he enjoyed their cool solitude. It was a pleasant sensation, he reflected, to be alone while surrounded by a thousand living things.

The leaves began to change colours, and Piers realized that winter was approaching. Parsifal would have to finish his training and do some great deeds quickly if they were to spend the cold months at King Arthur's Camelot, which Piers assumed every knight did. He was pondering this one afternoon when he heard the soft, continuous sound of falling water. Since Piers walked this way often and had never heard this sound before, he went to investigate.

Not fifty yards from Piers's usual path was a waterfall, one that had certainly not been there the day before, and in the shallow pool at the foot of the fall, a girl knelt and washed her hair. Piers hid behind a fallen tree that was covered with ivy and mistletoe and watched. The girl looked to be about his age. Her skin was fair, and she wore a simple white shift, but her hair was as black as pitch. Over the muted roar of the waterfall, Piers could hear brief musical strains as the girl sang to herself. The water where the girl knelt still came only up to her waist, and it was so clear that he could see her legs curled beneath her and even saw a fish swim by. The girl bent forward and dipped her head and hair all the way underwater. Then she straightened up swiftly, throwing her long hair in a smooth arc over her head and onto her back, revealing her face.

Piers had never seen a lovelier face, a pale oval set with two brilliant sapphires. He gasped, and the girl stood quickly, staring about her. Wearing his red hat, Piers was not difficult to find, and the girl uttered a faint shriek and backed away toward the waterfall.

"Please, don't go!" Piers heard himself saying. "I'm sorry I frightened you."

The girl hesitated, and for a long moment she looked into Piers's eyes. Her brow furrowed slightly, and she cocked her head to one side, but then she shook herself and ran through the falling water and disappeared. Piers scrambled over the fallen tree and ran around the pool to the side of the waterfall to look behind the veil of water. There was nothing there but rock.

And the next day there was no waterfall either. Piers sat in the clearing where the day before a beautiful girl had splashed in a crystal pool, and he tried to remember everything he had ever heard about the faeries. It was not much. The only faeries he had ever cared to hear stories about were the ones who helped knights on their quests, like the Lady of the Lake in some of the tales. Once, when he was very young, he had had a terrible nightmare about tiny sprites dancing about his bed and calling for him to get up and play, but then in the dream his father had appeared and sent the little people away with a word, and his mother had held him close and crooned softly to him until he felt better. Beyond these vague impressions of the faery world, he knew nothing.

Every day he returned to the spot of the vanished waterfall, hoping to find it again. After a few weeks, the details of the encounter seemed vague and formless, like his old nightmare, and he would have begun to believe that he had imagined it but for his vivid memory of the girl.

"I know I saw you," he said to the emptiness around him. "I'll never forget that. You were like something I had seen before, or had always wanted to see, but I just didn't know it." There was no answer but the chattering of a squirrel, and Piers returned to the hut of Jean le Forestier.

At dinner that night, Jean said, "It is time for you to go, Parsifal."

"Am I ready?" Parsifal asked. "You are still a far better swordsman and jouster than I. I could learn much more from you."

Jean nodded. "Yes, you could, but I have taught you enough to fight well. Now you must learn the rest by fighting different knights. No one who has fought against only one opponent can be truly skilled, for he has learned only one man's tricks and habits. You must go."

"I shall be beaten easily, I'm afraid," Parsifal said.

"No." Jean's whiskers twitched. "You may be beaten, but not easily. You are strong, you are faster than anyone I have ever trained, and you never make the same mistake twice. Someday you shall be famous. And besides, no one else – save only Arthur and one other – has a sword like yours. Yes, my dear friend, you are ready."

Parsifal nodded. "We shall leave in the morning."

Piers heard this exchange with mixed feelings. While he had been longing to depart almost since the moment they arrived, he suddenly realized that he did not want to leave the waterfall. When dinner was over, and Jean and Parsifal were stretched out before the fire, Piers slipped away and crept back into the woods for one last visit. The woods seemed different in the dark, but he had made the journey so many times that he had no trouble finding his way, and as he came near he was rewarded with the gentle sound of water. The waterfall was back. His heart pounding, he crept close to the waterfall, to the very edge of the pond, and gazed searchingly into the water.

The night was cold, and the spray from the fall wet him to the skin. Soon he was shivering uncontrollably, but still he stayed. He might have no other chance to see the girl again. Then, before his astonished eyes, the waterfall sank slowly into the ground. The grassy meadow bubbled like soup in a kettle and swallowed it. In a moment, it was gone and only his soaked clothing showed that it had ever been. Sadly, Piers turned and started to walk away.

"Please," said a quiet voice, "do not turn around."

Piers halted. "Who are you?" he whispered.

"My name is Ariel."

"Are you . . . the one I saw before?"

"Yes."

"What . . . I mean, who are you?"

"I am like you. But I live in another world, in the Seelie Court."

"The Seelie Court? Is that the court of the faeries?"

"It is. I have been permitted to see you again because I have a message for you."

"For me?"

"And for your master. Ride to water, Piers. Follow the water."

"What does that mean?"

There was no answer. Ariel was gone.

4

THE QUEEN OF BELREPEIRE

Piers and Parsifal rode northward, and just like before, Parsifal made no effort to spare the horses. As always, Piers rode in his correct subservient position, behind his master, but he began to wish he hadn't insisted on it quite so forcefully. It would make the long days in the saddle a little less tedious if they could talk. But, although Piers was often sore from riding, at least he was never hungry. Every night, Parsifal would go hunting, and he never returned empty-handed.

On the second day they left the forests behind and began to ride in more settled lands, and on the fifth day they came to a castle. Parsifal stopped his horse, and Piers decided to forget decorum this time and rode up beside him. Parsifal greeted him with a smile, then turned his attention to the castle.

"It seems deserted."

"There aren't any flags, even," Piers said, nodding. "No one is home."

"Let's go in and look. Maybe it's a great deed." They started forward, but before they had gone ten yards, there was a flurry of movement at the windows and on the walls, and a line of seven knights on gaunt horses came riding out toward them.

"How do you do?" Parsifal said, when the knights were close enough to hear. "I hope you are well today."

The knight in the middle said abruptly, "Go away."

Parsifal frowned, then said simply, "But I've done nothing to you."

The knight replied. "Nor shall you. We are seven and you are two. Leave now or be slain."

Piers caught his breath and began to edge his horse backwards, but Parsifal only put on his helm and said, "No."

"Psst!" Piers hissed. "I don't think there are any great deeds in that castle. Why don't we try somewhere else?"

Parsifal shook his head and, reaching back on his saddle, drew his lance from its fastenings. He pointed the lance at the knight who had spoken, who promptly fainted and fell off his horse. Parsifal raised his visor, looked at the man, then back at Piers. "Do you think I frightened him?" he asked.

Two of the other knights dismounted and hurried to the unconscious man on the ground, but another rode his horse a step forward and said gruffly, "You still must go away! She wants nothing to do with you!"

Parsifal ignored him, watching instead the two knights who were helping the man on the ground. They pulled his helm off, and Piers could only stare. He had never seen a thinner face. Parsifal replaced his lance on his saddle and dismounted. "Your friend is not well," he said calmly. "Pierre, bring my horse." Then Parsifal stooped, effortlessly lifted the unconscious man, and carried him toward the castle. Looking at each other helplessly, the other knights followed, and Piers brought up the rear.

They entered the castle, an odd procession, and were met in the courtyard by a tall woman with a firm chin and a direct gaze. She was a trifle thin, Piers noted, and her clothing hung loosely on her, but even so she was strikingly beautiful. Parsifal set the unconscious knight down in the courtyard, then stood and met the woman's gaze.

"He passed out," Parsifal said simply. "He looks to me as if he could use a good meal."

"So could we all," the woman said. "I thank you for bringing my captain back to us. It is an unlooked-for consideration."

"It was no trouble," Parsifal said. "We weren't busy anyway." He had not taken his eyes from the woman's face, and very slowly, a smile began to curl his mouth. "My name is Parsifal," he said, executing a flawless bow that Sir Gurnemains would have been thrilled to witness, "and I am your servant."

"Parsifal?" the woman said, her brows rising suddenly. "Then you are not... good gracious, are you not from King Clamide?"

Parsifal shook his head. "No. Who is King Clamide?"

The woman sighed with relief. "Oh, I am so sorry. We've been gravely inhospitable. My name is Conduiramour, and I am the Queen of Belrepeire, which is what we call this castle."

"Condwir..." Parsifal repeated hesitantly.

"Conduiramour," the queen said, a dimple showing on her pale cheek. "It's a frightful name, I know. My mother was French, and she thought it was cute. Do you speak French?" Parsifal shook his head, and the queen said, "It means something

66

like 'Love-bringer'. I honour my mother, but she was a bit of a loon sometimes. Please call me Connie."

Parsifal nodded mutely, his smile growing. Watching his master curiously, Piers suddenly realized that Parsifal was an amazingly handsome fellow. Queen Conduiramour's dimple appeared again.

"I would ask you to dinner, Sir Parsifal," the queen said, "but it won't be much I'm afraid. You see, King Clamide, the one I mentioned earlier, has decided that I should marry him, and so for the past few months he has seen to it that we have no food. His men occupy all of our farmland and have stolen all of our herds."

"So that's why your knight is so weak," Parsifal said.

The knight began to stir, and Queen Conduiramour knelt beside him. "Reynold, you impossible man. I thought I told you not to go out against anybody else."

"I was feeling much better," the knight muttered.

"I can tell," the queen said. "Thank you, Reynold. But as it turns out, it was all for nothing anyway. This knight isn't from Clamide at all."

With a struggle, the knight rose to his feet and

looked at Parsifal. "I'm glad to hear it. You looked like a nice chap. Sorry I braced you like that, but I couldn't have Queen Connie doing something silly."

"I'll decide what I do and whether it's silly or not, Reynold," the queen said reprovingly.

The knight looked down his nose at the queen. "You can use that tone of voice with someone else, my lady. Someone who didn't teach you to ride your first pony, perhaps. But if you plan to come high and mighty over me, I'll beg leave to go on about my business." Clicking his heels together sharply, he walked away toward the gate.

The queen sighed. "At least he didn't remind me that his wife used to change my nappies. It's a sad trial being surrounded by people who've known me since I was a child. You know, they wouldn't even tell me what Clamide was doing until they couldn't hide it any longer. They kept serving my dinners like always, while the rest of the castle was on half-rations, then quarter-rations. But forgive me for rattling on. Do come in. We can offer you nothing but a roof over your head, but that we do offer you, and gladly."

Parsifal did not move. "How many people are here?"

The queen hesitated, then lifted her chin and

said, "No more than thirty souls are left in the castle. And only seven knights."

Parsifal glanced over his shoulder at Piers. "The venison, Pierre."

Piers grinned and began emptying their saddlebags of all of the meat that they had carried with them since their last stop. It was little enough for thirty people, but it was still most of a young buck, and everyone could have a few bites. Queen Conduiramour's dimple grew deeper yet.

That night Queen Conduiramour and an elderly waiting woman sat in a small sitting room with Parsifal. Piers stood correctly behind Parsifal's chair, which made the queen lift her brows again.

"Please, friend, sit with us," she said to Piers.

Piers blushed, but he said, "I am comfortable here, your highness."

The queen glanced at Parsifal, and Parsifal shrugged. "Pierre is, ah, very correct." Piers could not tell, of course, but something in the slight movement of Parsifal's head made him suspect that Parsifal had rolled his eyes.

Queen Conduiramour chuckled. "As you wish, Pierre." She turned her attention to Parsifal. "So tell me about your adventures."

"My adventures?"

"Yes, of course. In my father's day, we held a banquet for every wandering knight and asked him to tell his adventures. My father died two years ago, and I'm afraid that the banquet is out of the question, but we can always hear adventures."

Parsifal laughed suddenly. "I'm afraid I've as much adventure to tell as you have banquet to share. We both are paupers."

"But this cannot be! Every knight had adventures to tell. Even if he'd never had any, he could make some up." She chuckled again. "And some of them were surely invented, too."

"Were they so unbelievable?"

"Unlikely, shall we say. When a skinny little fellow with bells on his shoes tells about defeating a giant, well, what is one to think?"

"Giants are not very difficult," Parsifal said. "But most are rather good-hearted. I shouldn't think anyone needed to fight one."

The queen laughed. "There, that's better. Have you known so many giants, then?"

"Oh no, only a few. I've known more of the little people than the big ones. You know, the faeries and elves and such."

Everyone in the room was quiet, staring at Parsifal, Piers most of all. He desperately wanted to ask his master if he knew anything about the

70

Seelie Court that Ariel had spoken of, but he held his tongue.

"Tell me about the little people," Queen Conduiramour said softly, her eyes bright.

"First you must tell me what I may do to help you," Parsifal said.

The queen's eyes clouded, and her face grew grave. "There is little that any one knight can do. King Clamide has won. He sent his men ahead of him to bottle us up, starve us out, weaken us. Most of my men deserted, which was just as well since their departure made what food we had last longer. Then yesterday Clamide sent a messenger saying that he would soon arrive himself to claim my hand in marriage, whether I gave it willingly or not."

"That does not sound like marriage to me," Parsifal said thoughtfully. "But perhaps there is more than one kind."

"There must be," Queen Conduiramour said ruefully. "But for my part, I think as you do. What he proposes is not marriage but slavery."

"That is why you must not do it, my lady!" the waiting woman sitting with her burst out. "Please reconsider!"

The queen shook her head. "No, Lisette. You have all declared yourselves my protectors. But I

71

am queen. I should be protecting you."

The woman sank on her knees in front of the queen's chair. "My lady, we would all consider it an honour to starve for your sake!"

"But I've no desire to rule over your noble corpses, you foolish woman. Sit up, Lisette. My mind is made up."

"From which direction did the messenger come?" Parsifal asked.

"From ... from the east, I believe, but why do you ask?"

"I was just wondering why I had never heard of this King Clamide before. But we've come from the south." Parsifal's voice was calm and even. "Shall I tell you about the little people now? There is one sprite – Peaseblossom is her name – who's always mislaying her wand. Well, one day I was hunting ..."

For the next two hours, Parsifal told story after story of the doings of the faeries. Piers learned that the Seelie Court was the world of the good faeries and the Unseelie Court the realm of the witches and ogres and monsters. As for the queen, the worry lines on her face faded as she watched Parsifal and listened to his tales, and Piers found himself inching around Parsifal's chair so as to be able to see his master's face better. He had never really wondered where Parsifal had come from, but now – unless Parsifal was making it all up – it appeared that Parsifal had lived much of his life in forests and glens where he had passed easily between the World of Men and another world, a world of enchantment. Something in Piers's soul stretched, as if he were reaching for something that lay just beyond his grasp, and he closed his eyes and saw again the fair girl Ariel as she had been just before she had disappeared in the waterfall. The fire burned down to coals, and then the coals faded, and then at last were dark, and the small party broke up.

It was still long before dawn when Parsifal shook Piers awake. "Pierre, I'm sorry to disturb you, but I need help with my armour. I thought I could do it myself, but it's harder in the dark than I had expected."

"Armour? Are we leaving?"

"But of course. We will ride east today, I think. I have a great desire to meet this King Clamide."

They met the vanguard of King Clamide's army before eight o'clock. Parsifal stopped his horse in the middle of the path and waited for the first knight to reach him.

"Get out of the way," the knight growled.

"Are you one of King Clamide's knights?" Parsifal asked.

"I am. Now be gone!"

"Which one is your master?"

The knight rode his horse right up to Parsifal and rested his hand on his sword hilt. "I said be gone, sirrah, or taste my sword."

With incredible swiftness, Parsifal reached over from his own saddle, grabbed the knight by the top and the bottom edges of his breastplate, then lifted him clean out of his saddle and held him high above his head. The other knights riding toward them stopped abruptly, and Piers's own mouth dropped open. "You should be more polite, knight," Parsifal said pleasantly. Then, still holding the knight over his head, Parsifal began to shake him roughly up and down. For a minute the knight yelled in protest and shouted for help, trying vainly to reach his sword, but after a while the knight's yells faded into whimpers, and his arms and legs began to flop limply. With a final heave, Parsifal tossed the knight to the ground, where he lay gasping, an untidy heap of armour on the path.

Parsifal's horse gave an audible sigh, and Parsifal laughed. "Sorry, old fellow. Were we a bit heavy?" He nudged the horse forward to where the next knight sat, awestruck, on his horse. "Which one is your master?" he repeated.

"He's in the black armour, sir, just behind us there. You can't miss him. He has a sort of blue and yellow plume on his helmet, and his horse is grey."

Another knight, sitting nearby, added, "And his shield is white with a black bear on the front, and he always has a blue standard tied to the tip of his lance."

"I think I should be able to find him now," Parsifal said. "Thank you very much for your help."

"No trouble at all, sir," the nearest knight said. "Happy to be of service."

Parsifal and Piers rode through the line of knights, and had no trouble finding the knight in black armour with the blue and yellow plume. Parsifal drew his lance from its lashings on his saddle and levelled it. "If you are on your way to the castle of Belrepeire, then please turn around and go home."

The knight stopped and stared. "Why should I?"

"It's not polite to ask impertinent questions," Parsifal said and charged. In a second, the knight was on the ground, a full ten feet behind his horse. "That's why you should go home," Parsifal added.

The knight leaped to his feet and drew his sword.

"You shall pay for that, you dog!"

Parsifal did not hesitate. Drawing his own sword, he slid easily from the saddle and took his position. The black knight charged, and Parsifal parried his blow, feinted to the left, then struck from the right. The force of his blow sent the black knight stumbling forward to his knees. "Surely you can move faster than that," Parsifal said.

With a strangled cry, the knight leaped to his feet again and turned, only to have his sword struck from his hand. Parsifal stepped back and let the knight pick up his sword. "You're much slower than Jean le Forestier," Parsifal commented. As soon as the black knight had his sword again, Parsifal lunged forward, struck the knight twice sharply on the helm. Then, while the echoes of the blows were still in the air, Parsifal stuck his own sword in the ground, lifted the black knight from the earth, and threw him into a ditch.

"Did Jean teach you that?" Piers asked. He hadn't watched very closely, but he didn't remember anyone being thrown around during the training sessions at the woodcutter's hut.

"No, I just thought of it myself," Parsifal replied, retrieving his sword.

The black knight charged again, more slowly this

time, and Parsifal easily deflected his blow, stepped out of the knight's path, and landed a solid kick on the black knight's backside. The knight lurched forward, fell, and the visor of his helm ploughed a furrow in the dust of the path. There were knights all around, watching, but not one made a sound. The black knight rose shakily to his feet. "I . . . have never been . . . defeated."

Parsifal struck twice. At the first blow, he cut right through the blade of the black knight's sword. The second blow struck the knight's helm and drove him to his knees. "Yes, you have," Parsifal said calmly.

The knight's helm showed a deep dent where Parsifal's sword had hit it. Piers wondered idly if that helm could ever be repaired. It looked like a good helm, and it would be a shame for it to go to waste. Parsifal stood over his defeated opponent, who bowed his head and remained on his knees. There was a long silence; then Parsifal glanced over his shoulder at Piers.

"Pierre?"

"Yes, sir?"

"Now what do I do?"

Piers hadn't thought about that. He searched his memory of his mother's stories and vaguely remembered tales of knights sending defeated enemies to pay homage to someone. He said so to Parsifal.

"Oh, that's a good idea." Parsifal turned back to the knight. "King Clamide, I command you to go—"

"I'm not King Clamide."

"What?"

"I'm not Clamide."

"But they told me you were."

"Who told you?"

"Some of the knights up ahead."

The knight removed his helm and scowled over his shoulder. "You didn't happen to get the names of the chaps who told you so, did you?"

"No. I'm sorry. But they did say this was King Clamide's army."

"Oh, it's Clamide's army, all right. But I'm not him. I'm Sir Kingrun, his seneschal."

Parsifal frowned. "Which one is Clamide, then?"

"He's not here yet. He's coming along with a second wave of cavalry. I was supposed to take possession of the castle and have everything set for his triumphal entry."

"Well, you can't do it now."

"You don't say," Sir Kingrun said, disgust in his face. "Look here, can I get up?"

Parsifal glanced at Piers. "What do you think?"

Piers shrugged. "Even if he's not Clamide, you did defeat him. You still ought to send him somewhere."

Parsifal nodded. "True. Sir Kingrun, I command you to go to Belrepeire and give honour to Queen Conduiramour."

"No, please," Sir Kingrun said quickly. "I've been laying siege to them for months. They'd kill me!"

Parsifal hesitated. "You think so?"

"Of course they would. Wouldn't you?"

"No."

"Well, I would. Can't you think of somewhere else for me to go?"

Parsifal glanced back again. "Pierre?"

"You could send him to Sir Gurnemains," Piers suggested.

Sir Kingrun choked. "That old fool? I'd rather you kill me yourself than make me bow down to him."

Parsifal smiled suddenly. "I've got it. I want you to go to King Arthur's court and do honour to the woman that Sir Kai slapped. I forget her name, so you'll have to ask around."

Sir Kingrun sighed. "Well, all right. I suppose I can do that. And who shall I say sent me?"

"My name is Parsifal." With an elegant bow,

Parsifal extended his hand and said, "I'm very pleased to make your acquaintance."

Sir Kingrun looked incredulously at Parsifal's outstretched hand. At last he reached out and shook it weakly. "Charmed, I'm sure," he muttered.

At Parsifal's command, Sir Kingrun took his whole troop of knights with him as he turned west toward Camelot. Piers and Parsifal continued east.

Piers edged his horse as close to Parsifal's as he could and still be behind him. "It looked as if you defeated him very easily," Piers commented.

Parsifal nodded. "Yes. He must not be a very skilled knight, for he was ridiculously slow."

"He said that he had never been defeated," Piers reminded his master.

"Then he can't have had many fights," Parsifal replied.

They met up with King Clamide's army about an hour later. Parsifal had remembered to get a description of the king's armour from Sir Kingrun – painted with gold and set with jewels – so this time he didn't have to stop anyone to ask directions. Instead, he simply pointed his lance and charged. The knights in the lead stopped so abruptly that some of them fell from their horses.

Others wheeled and turned, and a few even made an effort to get to their own lances, but by the time anybody was ready to receive a charge, Parsifal was already past. Piers, who had been taken by surprise as much as the knights, simply held on to his hat and followed in the wide wake that Parsifal was leaving behind him.

By the time Piers caught up, Parsifal had already sent a knight in gold armour crashing to the turf and was himself dismounting. "Before I bash you, let me make sure this time. You *are* King Clamide, aren't you?"

The gold knight rose to his feet, spluttering curses. "What the devil do you think you're doing?"

"I asked first. Are you King Clamide? I'm sorry that I have to ask, because I don't want to be rude, but last time I didn't ask, and by the time I found out it was just King Clamide's seneschal, I had already beaten him, and I'm afraid that might have been even ruder." Parsifal glanced at Piers, as if seeking his judgement, and Piers nodded. Probably beating up the wrong man was worse etiquette than asking too many questions.

"You say you beat my seneschal?" the gold knight asked.

"Yes, that's right. If you're King Clamide, that is.

Black armour with pretty plumes on top. He said his name was Kingrun."

"Kingrun has never been defeated in combat," King Clamide said.

"Yes, he said that, too, but I didn't believe him. Do you mean it's true?" The king nodded, and Parsifal shook his head slowly. "Well, I must say, I think he needs to get out more." Parsifal shrugged. "But that's not important now. I've come to tell you that Queen Conduiramour doesn't want to marry you, so you can go home now."

"Never!"

"Or you can fight me." Parsifal drew his sword.

The king glanced around at his confused army. "Well, are you just going to sit there?"

There was a long silence. At last one of the knights raised his visor and looked curiously at the king. "What would you have us do, your highness?"

"What would I—? Fight him, of course."

"No, you've misunderstood," Parsifal explained. "I've only challenged you. But if the others want to have a turn when I'm finished with you, I don't mind." He looked at the knight who had spoken. "Would you like to fight me after I've beaten your king?"

The knight shook his head. "No, that's quite all

right. You go ahead."

One by one, the knights drew back, leaving Parsifal and King Clamide alone in a wide circle. The king gulped audibly, began to draw his sword, then pushed it back into its sheath and knelt. "Oh, dash it all. Very well, I yield."

Parsifal stared. "Don't you even want to fight?"

The king removed his helm, revealing a boyish face with a thin beard and a sallow complexion. "I've been ill, you see, or I'd fight you in a shot. I had one of my bilious attacks just last night. Ask my doctor, if you don't believe me." This last was said to his knights as much as to Parsifal. "And I think you've broken one of my ribs with your lance. It hurts right here." He pointed at his side.

Parsifal looked at Piers. "What do you think?"

"I suppose it counts as defeating him, since you did knock him down. Send him to do honour to someone, I guess."

"Queen Connie?"

Piers considered this. "If you couldn't send the other one to her, I don't suppose you can send this one."

"I guess not. I'll send him to that lady at Arthur's court, too." For the next minute, Parsifal gave his directions to King Clamide. He made him promise to give up all pretension to Queen Conduiramour's hand, and sent him off with his army in his train.

"Before we go back," Parsifal said, "let me get us some fresh meat."

They came back to Belrepeire just at dusk. The gates were shut, but when Parsifal called out, the elderly knight Sir Reynold opened the gate. Sir Reynold looked carefully about him. "Welcome back, sir," he said. "We thought you had left us."

"I did, but I'm back," Parsifal said. "May I see the queen?"

Queen Conduiramour herself stepped out of the shadows. "Welcome home, Parsifal. I was disappointed when they said you had left during the night."

Parsifal dismounted and walked up to the queen. "I didn't want to wait here, because I was afraid that King Clamide might kill me, and I didn't think that would be pleasant for you to watch, so I went on up the road."

Queen Conduiramour's brow creased. "On up the road?"

"Yes, so that when I fought them I'd be out of sight."

"You fought them?"

"That's right. But as it turned out, I could have fought them here just as well. I don't think that

King Clamide really has much stomach for fighting after all. Of course, he wasn't feeling well, and one must take account of illness. You know how weak it can make you feel. But even that other fellow, what was his name, Pierre?"

"Sir Kingrun."

"Yes, even Sir Kingrun was disappointing. Anyway, I sent them off, so you can have your farmlands back. And here are three deer and a boar. If you like, we could roast them all together tonight. It would be like a celebration."

Queen Conduiramour's face brightened and softened, and a huge smile spread across it. "Just like a celebration," she said softly. Parsifal smiled at her, and then the queen reached up and took Parsifal's face in her hands and kissed him soundly on the lips.

Parsifal gaped at her for a second, then said hesitantly, "My mother told me that one day I would see a woman I thought more fair than any other, and that I should kiss her."

"Your mother was very wise, Parsifal," the queen said, and they kissed again.

5

THE CASTLE
THAT WASN'T THERE

The problem, Piers thought as he paced the floor in his room at Belrepeire, was that it had all happened too fast. It was almost three months since he and Parsifal had first come to Belrepeire, and fully two months after Parsifal and Queen Conduiramour had been married, and Piers still had the feeling that something had gone wrong.

He pushed out his lips in what his mother used to call a *moue*. It wasn't that he disapproved of Queen Conduiramour. She was, as far as he could tell, the perfect lady. She was wise and graceful, beautiful and witty, quick with both her laughter and her sympathy, beloved by all her subjects, and very clearly in love with Parsifal. It was just that – Piers frowned and tried to put it into words – it was just that she had appeared on the scene too early. In his mother's stories, the beautiful maiden who marries the hero had always appeared at the *end* of the story, after years of trials and many great victories. But in this case, Parsifal had had six months of training under Sir Gurnemains and Jean le Forestier, and then, within weeks, had saved the lady and married her and become King of Belrepeire. How could you become a king before you've even become a knight? There just wasn't anything like it in the stories.

Forcing himself to be honest, Piers admitted that a part of his dissatisfaction was that he was bored. He had dreamed of being the page of a great king, and so he was, he supposed, but it was not at all what he had expected. He had imagined a life of glamour and great banquets and balls every night and had pictured himself carrying private messages from knights to their secret loves and being a part of castle intrigues. Compared to that image, life at Belrepeire was sadly flat. Parsifal and the queen ate the same simple meals as their servants, and neither showed much interest in ceremony. They often went out to their tenants' farms to visit their subjects. Parsifal still went hunting often, and he had even gone out with some of the castle servants to cut wood when their supply got low. A king who would take an axe out with his woodcutters was not the type who required much service from a page. Parsifal ran his own errands, sent no secret love letters, and even chose his own clothes. Once again, it didn't fit the stories, and Piers simply couldn't account for it.

Once or twice, when Piers was alone with Parsifal, he had delicately suggested that perhaps he and the queen would like to make a state visit to Camelot to see King Arthur, or one of the lesser kings in England, like King Mark of Cornwall. Even that would be interesting, Piers thought, because although King Mark was reputed to be a surly fellow, the famous Sir Tristram was in Cornwall. Piers would dearly love to meet some of the knights he had heard of in the stories.

Piers sighed and closed his window. It was only about five o'clock, but Parsifal and the queen ate their dinner unfashionably early, and one of the few jobs that Piers actually had was to serve their meal. He walked down to the kitchens, where the cook was dishing up a plain mutton stew with bread. Piers shook his head as he lifted the tray. To see such a common meal set before royalty would have broken Sir Gurnemains's heart.

Parsifal and his queen were sitting in the small dining room where they usually took their meals when Piers arrived. They were silent, which struck Piers as odd, because usually they were talking and laughing together when he arrived. Beyond a quiet, "Thank you, Pierre," neither spoke to him. Piers withdrew to his usual place at the wall, and watched with growing consternation as the two ate almost their entire meal in silence. At last, as he pushed away his empty bowl, Parsifal spoke.

"Look, Connie, I *am* happy here."

Queen Conduiramour's voice was soft. "I had always thought so."

"And I *will* come back," Parsifal said firmly. Piers stared, suddenly intent on his master.

"But you won't say when?"

"I can't, Connie. I don't know when. It may take me a while to convince my mother to leave her home and join us here."

"And what if she won't? What if she wants you to stay? What will you do?"

"I will come back to you, Connie. I love you."

The queen looked at her half-finished meal for a moment, and when she looked back up, her eyes were bright with tears but she smiled. "I know, Parsifal. But I can't help feeling that there's some other reason that you want to leave."

This time it was Parsifal who hesitated before answering. "Maybe there is." He stood and walked to the window, looking down on the fields below, just as Piers had been doing twenty minutes before. "It is only that . . . I left my mother and my home because I wanted to be a knight. I wanted to have adventures and do great deeds. I have done nothing."

"You saved me and the castle," Queen Conduiramour exclaimed.

"But it was too easy! The first knight fought poorly, and King Clamide did not fight at all. I won your victory without even trying. Should I not face some difficult tests before I settle into life with you?"

The queen looked sadder than ever, but she nodded. "I was afraid it might be that. You are king of this land, but I have noticed that you do not like to be called king."

"This is your kingdom, Connie. I want to earn my own titles."

"Then you must go," the queen said softly. "And I will miss you every day."

"And I will miss you," Parsifal said, taking her hand. He glanced over his shoulder at Piers.

"You coming with me, Pierre?"

"Yes, sir!" Piers said, delighted. Then, remembering that Parsifal's departure was a cause of sorrow to the queen, he quickly moderated his glee and, searching his memory for something suitable to say, added, "Your highness?" Queen Conduiramour looked at him. "Forgive me, your highness, but it is a noble thing that you do. He could not love you, queen, so much, loved he not honour more."

Queen Conduiramour and Parsifal looked at each other in silence for a moment, then dissolved in helpless laughter. Piers flushed and stood rigid until they had regained control of themselves. "Forgive us, Pierre," the queen said, "we meant no disrespect, but really, have you any notion how stupid that sounded?"

Not wanting to prolong their goodbyes, Piers and Parsifal left the next morning, heading east. "How long will it take us to get to your mother's home?" Piers asked.

"I don't know," Parsifal answered. "I don't even know which direction to take. You see, when I came here to look for King Arthur, I came from the Other World."

"What do you mean?"

"Where my mother lives, there are many doors to the Other World – the World of Faeries – and I often travelled there. It was in that world that I saw my first knight."

"There are knights in the Other World?"

"Not usually," Parsifal explained. "But this was a knight of King Arthur's court who was on a quest. I wrestled with him and then gave him directions."

"What knight of Arthur's court?" Piers asked, interested.

"I never asked his name. Anyway," Parsifal continued. "I went home to my mother to tell her that I wanted to be a knight. She did not want me to, but at last she consented, and I went back to the Other World to look for this knight I had met. I didn't find him, but instead, I found a new doorway to the World of Men. It took me right to Arthur's camp, where we met."

Piers licked his lips. He had ridden up almost alongside Parsifal in his eagerness to hear more about the Other World, and he felt that he ought to return to his subservient position, but he had one more question to ask, one that he had not dared to ask in anyone else's presence. "Parsifal, in all your travels in the Other World, did you ever meet a faery named Ariel?"

Parsifal considered the question. "Male or female?"

"Female. About my age, I think."

Parsifal looked at Piers sharply. "You think? Do

you mean that you've seen this faery?"

Piers nodded. "Unless it was a dream," he added.

"It hardly matters if it was," Parsifal replied. He smiled broadly. "I would not have thought it of you. You seem so much a part of this world that I should never have expected you to see one of the Others. No, Pierre, I know of no girl named Ariel in that world. Perhaps you can introduce me to her someday."

"If I see her again," Piers said glumly.

"I shouldn't worry about that," replied Parsifal.

They rode over a small hill and from the summit looked down on a pond that was fed by a small stream. In the pond were two men, fishing from a little ketch. One of the men, reclining in the stern, was wearing the most splendid purple clothing that Piers had ever beheld, more magnificent than anything at Arthur's court or at Sir Gurnemains's castle. Parsifal led the way to the edge of the pond.

"How do you do, sir," Parsifal said. "I hope you are well today."

"I hope so, too," the man in purple said, very softly. "Have you come far?"

"Not so very far," Parsifal said. "I am looking for great deeds to do."

The man in the boat grimaced slightly, as if having a spasm of pain, and the other man in the boat said, "Dip your wrists in the water, Nuncle. It always gives you relief."

The man in purple did so and seemed to rest easier. He turned to Parsifal and said, "I do not know what you consider a great deed, but you may ask at the castle that is behind that hill there."

"Thank you, sir, I will," Parsifal said politely. "Behind that hill."

"Yes. Just follow the water," the man said, sinking slowly back into the stern of the boat.

Parsifal rode alongside the small stream toward the hill. When they were past the two anglers, he looked back at Piers. "Do you think that man was ill?"

"I wondered, too," Piers said, "but I'm glad that you didn't ask. Some people are very sensitive about their ailments. He could have been offended."

"Oh, I haven't forgotten *everything* that you and Sir Gurnemains taught me," Parsifal said lightly.

The hill toward which the fisherman had pointed was not very large around, but was quite tall – a sharp plug of rock jutting up from the ground. When Piers and Parsifal came round it, Piers saw to his surprise that the hill must be larger than it appeared, for behind it was a castle more magnificent than anything he had ever imagined.

The two travellers stared. "Surely there are great deeds to do in such a place as that," Parsifal said eagerly.

They clopped over a tiny bridge and entered the castle gate. Three ladies stood in the entrance hall. "Welcome, sir," one said. "We have been waiting for you. I am bid to bring you to your rooms and thence to the feast."

"Feast?" Parsifal said. He leaned forward as if to ask more, but at the last second caught himself. He glanced at Piers and grinned ruefully. "You are very kind," he said to the lady.

The ladies led them to a large bedchamber and left them, promising to send someone for them soon. Piers helped Parsifal remove his armour. "This is mysterious, isn't it, Pierre?"

"Very," Piers assented.

"I think they have some secret here," Parsifal said firmly. "I can feel the magic of it." He pondered this for a moment, then added, "But I imagine that they'll tell us what it is when they're ready." Piers nodded his approval and surveyed his master. Even coming straight from a long ride, Parsifal looked fresh and elegant. Piers was proud of him.

A slight tapping came from the door, and then an impish face peeked in. Piers recognized the man who had been in the boat with the magnificent fisherman. "Yes?" Parsifal asked.

"Oo, ye're not up to much, are ye?" the man said, wrinkling his face. He stepped into the room, and Piers saw that he was wearing the motley multi-coloured garb of a royal fool. "I was thinking ye'd be so grand, but here ye be, a mere sprat of a boy." He reached across and patted Piers's head. "Ye looked bigger in yere armour, son."

Piers stepped back distastefully, and Parsifal said, "*I* was the one in the armour, fellow."

"Ah, that's better, think on. But even so. . . " The man turned his scrutiny to Parsifal. "Ye don't look like so much yereself. Can ye do this?" With a sudden leap, the man flipped himself over into a handstand and began walking around the room on his arms, clucking like a chicken.

Piers and Parsifal stared at the man with consternation, but they said nothing. At last the man righted himself, looked back at the two and said, "Nay, ye're neither one worth a dram. 'Twere better if ye'd never come. Ye haven't even asked my name or my business."

Parsifal replied with dignity. "I assume that your business is to lead us to the feast. As for your name, I care not what to call such a frivolous fellow."

Piers felt himself swell with pride, and he wished Sir Gurnemains had been present to hear his pupil reply so masterfully to this impertinent jester. The man stuck his tongue out and made the rude gesture called a "fig" at Parsifal, but then he turned on his heel and led the way out the door. Piers and Parsifal followed, and in a few minutes were led into a grand banquet hall filled with people in gorgeous raiment.

"I've brought them in, Nuncle," the man shouted. "For all the bleeding good they'll be. 'Twill all be for nought, I fear me."

Piers followed the man's eyes and saw at the head of a long table, propped up by pillows on a dais, the fisherman who had directed them to the castle. The fisherman wore a gold circlet on his forehead, a crown. With a slight wave, the fisherman king beckoned to Parsifal and waved him into a seat beside the dais. Parsifal took his seat, and Piers assumed his position behind Parsifal's chair.

"I am glad that you've come," the fisherman king said. His voice was grainy and weak. Ladies and courtiers who were gathered all around looked at him anxiously. One lady, who had an air of authority, waved an arm toward the great open door at the other end of the hall, and then began the strangest procession Piers had ever seen.

First, through the door walked a page, about Piers's age, carrying a long lance. As they drew close, Piers saw with horror that the point of the lance was streaming with blood, as if the blood were welling out of the lance itself. The fisherman king closed his eyes and looked away, then nodded. The page gently pointed the lance at the fisherman king's upper thigh. Looking hard, Piers thought he could see blood on the fisherman king's clothing there. Then, with a firm thrust, the page pushed the point of the lance into the king's leg. Fresh blood welled up from a wound, the king grimaced with pain, and Parsifal started to rise from his chair in alarm, but then the king relaxed. The page withdrew, and the king seemed to breathe more easily.

Before Piers had time to wonder about what he had just witnessed, two young girls came whirling wildly into the room. They seemed to be dressed entirely in flowers, and flower petals flew from their fingertips as they danced. A sweet perfume filled the hall. The girls left a shower of petals on the fisherman king and then disappeared behind him. Following on their heels, but walking much more sedately, came four regal ladies in matching white robes, each carrying a lit candelabrum.

Parsifal, who had reluctantly settled himself back

in his chair leaned toward Piers. Piers inclined his head. "Do you think they'll explain all this later?" Parsifal whispered.

"I don't know," Piers replied. He was urgently curious himself. He wanted desperately to ask for an explanation.

Parsifal took a deep breath, then whispered, "If they don't tell us tonight, then tomorrow I will have to ask." Piers nodded vigorously. It was a good compromise, he decided, between good manners and good sense.

The ladies with the candelabra stood on the dais with the fisherman king, and two more ladies appeared, these in gowns that shone like silver, and they each bore a long, glittering knife. Piers could not look away from the two knives. At a glance he knew that they were perfectly balanced and from the glint on the edge he decided that they were sharp enough to slice a man's finger to the bone before he'd even felt the cut. They shone more brightly than any steel he'd ever seen at his father's forge, and he realized with a start that these knives must be made of silver. The hafts of the knives, or at least the part that showed beneath the ladies' hands, were curiously wrought with delicate metalwork that Piers longed to examine more closely. Had Parsifal not decided to ask for explanations in the morning, Piers would have been unable to restrain his need to know more about these brilliant blades.

Finally, one last lady entered, bearing something on an earthen tray. Piers stared, but he could not tell exactly what it was: the woman carried it on a tray as if it were a vessel of some sort, but it seemed to Piers more like a simple stone, roughly and irregularly cut, of the sort that anyone might find tossed aside by workmen at a quarry. The lady laid the stone on the table before the fisherman king, who sighed, looked once at the object, then lay back on his pillow and went to sleep.

Parsifal and Piers looked once more into each other's eyes, though neither spoke. The rest of the assembled company began to cry, sobbing softly. There was now food on the table, which had simply appeared when the stone was placed there. Parsifal hesitated, but no one made any movement to eat, and so, after waiting another moment, he took some food and quietly ate while everyone else wept.

Perhaps there was magic in the food, or else in the perfume from the scattered flowers, but Piers could barely hold his eyes open after the feast was finished. Neither he nor Parsifal attempted to discuss the strange sights they had witnessed, but instead both fell heavily into their beds, and when Piers opened his eyes, the sun had already risen.

He sat up and rubbed his eyes. There was no sound but a faint whistling of wind through chinks in the castle wall. Piers stretched and threw back his covers. The fire that had warmed the room when he had gone to sleep was nothing but cold, gray ashes, and Piers dressed hurriedly and threw his warm travelling cloak around himself to ward off the chill.

"Is it already day?" Parsifal asked, sitting up.

"Yes," Piers said. "And no one has come in to build the fire in the room this morning. Strange notion of hospitality they have in this castle."

"Strange customs all around," Parsifal said, swinging his feet to the cold stone floor. "Let's get dressed and go find someone to ask about last night."

"Yes, let's," Piers said. Parsifal pulled on his warm clothes and then, because they didn't know if they would be coming back to the room, Piers helped him put on his armour and belt on his sword. They left the room together.

"Hello!" Parsifal called. There was no answer. He called again, and still got no reply. The castle was as still as a crypt. "Is no one awake yet?" Parsifal asked. They found their way to the courtyard, which was empty, and from there found the stables. There were their own horses, but no others. The castle was completely deserted.

"Maybe everyone's out hunting or . . . or something, outside the walls," Piers suggested tentatively. They saddled their horses and led them out of the stables, their ears straining for any sound that they did not make themselves. They heard none.

"Let's go see," Parsifal said, and they rode out the castle gates. Immediately the portcullis slammed shut behind them, and the great oaken doors closed. Piers and Parsifal turned in their saddles and watched, amazed and uncomprehending.

"I told them ye'd be worth naught!" shouted a voice. It was the man in motley who had taken them to the banquet room. He stood on the wall over the gate, looking at them from the battlements. "Why couldn't ye ask, ye blithering gapeseeds? Why wouldn't ye say the words, even? Ye had it in yere hands to bring it all back to rights, but ye said nothing! Ye said nothing when ye saw the lance – tell me, ye wise fools, when ye've ever seen sich a lance as that? Ye wouldn't ask about the knives of Trebuchet, and then – ah, asses that ye are! – ye wouldn't ask even when ye saw the Grail itself!"

"The Grail?" Parsifal shouted back. "What is that?"

"Shut up!" the man screamed, dancing with rage. "Do ye think I've time for yere questions now? Why couldn't ye ask when it was time? Why couldn't ye even ask about King Anfortas? Ah, but ye never even knew his name did ye, the noblest king ever born, and do you know why ye didn't know his name? Because ye didn't ask!"

"I did not think it polite to be forever asking questions," Parsifal said. "Of course I wanted to know."

"Nay! 'Tis a lie! Had ye wanted to know, ye would have asked! The one who asks no questions only wants others to think him clever! Fools! Blockheads! Fatheaded dolts!" At that, the man disappeared behind the wall.

With a low moan, Parsifal spurred his horse and began to gallop along the stream, around the hill, back toward the pond where they had first seen the fisherman king. Piers followed, but no one was there. "No!" Parsifal shouted. He wheeled his horse and raced back toward the castle. But when they came back around the hill, the castle was gone. Only a field of thin, early spring grass was in the place where the castle had been.

Parsifal was silent and brooding, and in truth Piers was glad of it. He was in no mood to talk either. A huge weight had descended on him, and everything he looked at seemed edged in a dark outline that he had never noticed before. He sensed, in a way that he had never sensed anything before, that a great opportunity had just presented itself, and he had let it go. His mother had always made the life of a page sound so splendid, but it was not splendid to fail. And though he could not say exactly how he had done it, he knew he had failed.

Ahead of him, Parsifal stopped suddenly, cocked his head as if to listen, then walked his horse forward. Piers heard nothing at first, but then made out the sound of a woman crying. They rounded a bend on the forest path, and came upon a woman with long, tangled hair, mounted on a staggering, spavined old mare. The woman's clothes were little more than rags, and huge holes gaped on every side, revealing red, chapped flesh. When Parsifal rounded the bend, though, the woman sat up straight and tried vainly to pull her torn garment around her to cover herself. She must have known how futile this pathetic effort at modesty was, but she tried all the same.

Parsifal slowly approached the woman, reaching behind him to his saddlebag as he rode. "My lady," he said. His voice was gentle. "Permit me to give you this cloak. I am afraid you will be cold."

The woman shook her head abruptly. "No!" she whispered. "Please go away! If he sees you, he'll kill you."

"I don't know who you mean," Parsifal said. "But it little matters. Here, take the cloak."

"I cannot! If he sees that I've taken a cloak from someone, from another man, then—"

The woman broke off as a knight in ill-kept armour galloped madly out of the forest. "Aha!" the knight shouted. "I've caught you again! Consorting with another of your paramours!"

"No, no," the woman gasped, sobbing.

"Do you know this woman?" Parsifal asked the furious knight.

"Know her? She is my wife!" the knight screamed. Through his open visor, Piers could see froth on the man's lips.

"If so, you should take better care of her," Parsifal said grimly. "She is cold, and she has little to wear."

"I make no doubt you've gazed your fill at her, along with every other man who meets her. It is no more than she wants! She is a trollop, a wanton! She is friend to every man but her own husband!"

"No, I swear it is not true," the woman said pitifully. "It was all innocent!"

"You gave your lover my ring, didn't you?" the knight shouted. "The ring I had myself given you just two days before!"

"I swear I did not, my love," the woman cried. "He took it from my finger! He was a youth, ill-mannered and too foolish to know what he was doing!"

Parsifal was forgotten as the knight raged at his wife. "But you admit that he kissed you! Do you not?"

"Yes, my lord, he did. But he was too fast for me. I could not stop him!"

"Ha!" the knight snapped. He turned back to Parsifal. "Have you ever heard such a story? She claims that while she was awaiting me in a grand pavilion, set with a feast for my dinner, a strange knight came upon her, ate of my feast, kissed her, and took my ring from her finger. And in all this she was innocent! Doxy!"

The heaviness that had pressed on him all morning became almost unbearable to Piers as he looked more carefully at the ragged woman and, with difficulty, recognized the lady that Parsifal had encountered on their second day after leaving King Arthur. Parsifal reached into his saddlebag and drew out the ring that he had taken from the woman that day. "This ring?" he asked.

The knight screamed with inhuman fury and threw himself at Parsifal, drawing his long sword as he spurred his horse. Parsifal did not move until the knight was almost on him; then he caught the man's sword arm in one hand and grasped the man's armour with the other and threw him from his saddle. Then Parsifal dismounted deliberately and drew his own sword. "The woman speaks the truth," he said slowly. "I was young and did not understand about women. I meant her no harm, and I did nothing more than what she has said."

The knight scrambled to his feet, and his sword flashed toward Parsifal, but Parsifal parried it and stepped away. "This woman has been true to you, I say. I was a fool and made a mistake."

The knight attacked again and was turned aside again. He said fiercely, "And for that mistake you shall die."

"Maybe. Or perhaps you shall die for your mistake. I am in no mood to endure one such as you." Parsifal began to level his own attack.

Everywhere the knight moved, Parsifal was there with a flashing sword or a heavy fist. Within five minutes he had knocked the strange knight down a dozen times. "Have you treated your wife this way ever since that day?" The knight did not answer, but Parsifal continued as if he had said yes. "That has been nine months, friend. I would kill a man for treating a dog in such a manner for so long. Have you any final words?"

The knight flailed weakly at Parsifal, who knocked his blade aside with a careless wave of his free hand and then struck a crashing blow on the knight's helm that sent him stumbling to the path.

"Madam, do you want me to kill this cur?" Parsifal said, raising his sword over his head.

"No! Please, no!"

"Why not?" Parsifal asked, his voice cold.

"I love him!"

Parsifal lowered his arm and looked at the woman. "Then you are a fool, madam. But for your sake, I will spare him." He looked back at the kneeling knight. "What is your name, you pig vomit?"

"I am Duke Orilus, and this is my wife, Lady Jeschute."

"Well, Duke Orilus, you are a vicious beast, and now you are a vicious beast who has been beaten.

Know now that your wife was faithful to you and that you still breathe only because of her love. Get up." Orilus staggered to his feet, and Parsifal threw him roughly back into his saddle.

"Go to King Arthur's court, to the lady whom Sir Kai struck, and do honour to her. Then tell your story to the king, and tell it true, or I will hear, and I will hunt you down and kill you with my hunting spears, like the mad swine that you are. Go!"

Duke Orilus and Lady Jeschute began to ride slowly away, and Parsifal looked over his shoulder at Piers. "Go with them, Pierre. I want no more to do with pages." And then Parsifal leaped on his horse and rode away, and Piers was left without a master, without a position, without a dream, and a sorrow like none he had ever known settled on his shoulders and he wept.

6

MALCHANCE, OBIE, AND OBILOT

Duke Orilus, Lady Jeschute, and Piers rode southwest toward Camelot, but a chance-met traveller told them that the king and his knights had gone to observe the Easter feast at Winchester, so they turned due south instead. For most of the ride, Piers was lost in his own sombre reflections, but he couldn't help noticing his companions to some degree. By the time they found King Arthur's camp, Piers was amazed to see that Orilus and Jeschute had forgiven each other everything and were behaving like newlyweds. They made him feel ill.

Duke Orilus had no trouble gaining an audience with the king, and so for the second time, Piers found himself in the presence of the hero of

England, wishing that he were elsewhere. Duke Orilus knelt before the king and said, "My liege, I come as I have been sent."

"Sent by whom?" the king asked.

"I know not, my liege. It was a red knight, of surpassing strength and skill. He has sent me here first to do honour to a lady, the lady who was struck by Sir Kai."

"Oh," King Arthur said. "Another one." The news clearly did not please him.

A knight with a wild red beard was sitting beside the king, and at Orilus's words, he looked up with surprise. "Eh? What's the tale here?"

King Arthur glanced at the knight. "Lady Connoire," he said. "While you were up north, she and Kai had a, ah, disagreement. She struck Kai, and he struck her back."

"Kai hit her?" the knight asked. "Was he drunk?"

"I was as surprised as you, nephew." The king glanced behind the red-bearded knight at a squire. "Terence, do you know where the Lady Connoire is?"

"I'll find her, sir. Bring her here?"

Arthur nodded, then looked back at the red-bearded knight. "As luck would have it, a country fellow was here wanting to be made a knight and he saw Kai do the deed. Well, that fellow – Peredur, or something like that – went and got himself some red armour. A few months later we got a couple of knights at court who had been defeated by the red knight and sent by him to do honour to Lady Connoire. Put Kai in a black mood for a week."

"I'll bet," the red-bearded knight said, grinning.

The king sighed. "I do wish the fellow – Parzisomething – would stop sending his used opponents to Lady Connoire, though. Dash it, what was his name?"

Piers, who had been standing behind Lady Jeschute, stepped into the open and bowed deeply. "Your highness?"

The king looked at him with surprise. "Yes, lad?"

"The knight you're thinking of – his name is Parsifal."

The red-bearded man leaped to his feet. "Parsifal?" he asked quickly.

King Arthur raised his eyebrows. "What is it, Gawain?"

Piers gasped. This man was the great Sir Gawain, of whom so many tales were told! To look on Gawain was almost as overwhelming as to look on Arthur himself.

"I may know the fellow," Sir Gawain said. "But

it's been years since we met, in...in a different country. We wrestled each other one night."

Piers nodded quickly. "Yes, sir. He told me that. He said that he met a knight in...in a different country, as you said, and that they wrestled and then he gave the knight some directions. Was that you, sir?"

"It was," Sir Gawain said. "And he came to become a knight after all, did he?"

King Arthur had been gazing intently at Piers. "Say, I know that red hat. Aren't you the page who brought Sir Ither's challenge to me?"

Piers knelt. "Yes, sire. I did so unwillingly."

"Yes, I remember that. Have you been with this Parsifal since then?"

"Yes, your highness. I was with him when he saved Queen Conduiramour and the Castle Belrepeire, and I was with him when he defeated Duke Orilus. He is, I think—" Piers hesitated, then continued with conviction, "When he is knighted, he will be a great knight."

"Then someone must find him and tell him to come and be knighted," King Arthur said mildly. "I wonder, Gawain, if..."

"It would be an honour, sire. I'll find him, in this or any other country he travels to."

Piers's heart was pounding, and he said, "Sir

Gawain?" The knight looked at him. "Please, sir, would you let me travel with you?"

Sir Gawain frowned. "I already have a squire, friend."

"Please. I have to tell Parsifal something." Sir Gawain looked a question, and Piers said, "I must tell him that I was wrong."

Sir Gawain reached out and flipped Piers's cheek carelessly. "All right, lad. What's your name?"

Piers lifted his chin and spoke clearly. "My name is Piers."

Even in his despondency, oppressed by his need to find Parsifal, Piers could not help feeling some excitement at setting out on a quest with the famous Sir Gawain. Sir Gawain rode in the lead atop the largest horse Piers had ever seen, followed by his silent squire, Terence. Piers rode last, determined to watch Terence's every move so as to learn how to serve a knight well.

He soon saw more than he'd expected. As soon as they were out of sight of the king's camp, Terence stopped his horse. Glancing over his shoulder, Sir Gawain reined in as well. "I can't leave you alone for a minute, can I?" Terence said in an irritated voice. Piers blinked in amazement.

"Oh, have you decided to stop giving me the

silent treatment?" Sir Gawain replied. "Well, then, let me explain what—"

"All I do is run one little errand, and what happens? I come back and find that you've volunteered to go off on a silly chase, looking for a knight. Shouldn't be hard, should it? He's only one knight and England's only one country. Whatever possessed you, milord?"

"Look, Terence, I'm sorry about this, but when I tell you—"

"Didn't it occur to you that I might be tired of travelling. Didn't it occur to you that I hadn't seen Eileen in a month and was looking forward to—"

"I have to, Terence!"

"Have to? Why do you have to look for this nameless knight?"

"He's not nameless! It was when I heard his name that I realized I needed to find him."

Terence's eyes widened. "Don't tell me it's your knock-brained brother again! I won't go off looking for Gareth, milord, and you shouldn't either. He'll just get lost again anyway."

"It's not Gareth," Sir Gawain said patiently. "His name's Parsifal."

"Parsifal? I don't know any... Parsifal, you say?" Terence hesitated. "You don't mean the chap you fought that night in the—" Terence broke off and glanced behind him at Piers for the first time.

"In the Other World," Piers supplied. Terence's eyes showed a sudden interest in the page.

"That's what I was trying to tell you," Sir Gawain said, while Terence scrutinized Piers. "This is Piers, Parsifal's former page, and he knew about that wrestling bout. So now you see why I had to volunteer, don't you? I'm the one who told Parsifal to come to Arthur's court in the first place." Sir Gawain paused, then added in a formal tone, "But if you don't want to come with me, of course, my lord duke, you could always stay behind."

Terence glanced at his master and snorted. "Milord, I know it's hard for you, but *do* try not to be more of an ass than God made you."

Sir Gawain laughed and started his horse again. Terence smiled at Piers, who was shocked at the familiar banter between the knight and his squire. Terence jerked his head. "Sorry I was out of sorts just now, Piers. Come ride beside me." And then Terence joined Sir Gawain, and to his own amazement Piers found himself riding between them, side by side, chatting easily with both.

Gawain began to question Piers about Parsifal. "The thing I'm wondering, lad, is how your friend is defeating all these knights. Arthur called him a country fellow. Has he received some training?"

"Yes, sir," Piers said. "After we left King Arthur, Parsifal studied for three months at the castle of one Sir Gurnemains."

The effect of this revelation was not what Piers had expected. Sir Gawain and Terence roared with laughter. "Not old Griflet's mentor!" Sir Gawain said between gasps. "And exactly what did Parsifal learn from that silly old fop?"

Piers flushed and looked down. "Manners, mostly," he muttered. Then he grinned at a sudden memory and added, "And how to walk funny."

"Well, manners are useful," Sir Gawain said, still grinning. "Just not in battle."

"Then, when we left Sir Gurnemains, Parsifal spent another three months training with sword and lance," Piers added, hoping that Sir Gawain would not ask any further questions. It was no use, though.

"Training with whom?" Sir Gawain asked.

Piers sighed. "With a woodcutter," he admitted.

Terence laughed suddenly, but not with the disdain that Piers had expected. "A woodcutter, you say. Would this woodcutter be named Jean le Forestier?" he asked. Piers nodded, and Terence grinned broadly.

"Do you know this Jean, Terence?" Sir Gawain

demanded. Terence nodded but did not offer any further explanation, and Sir Gawain turned back to Piers. "Tell me about him."

"I think Jean might not be his real name," Piers said. "I think he might once have been a squire or knight's servant, because he had his own sword hidden away. He was a big fellow with a wild beard and a bit of a French accent."

"French accent – Good Gog!" Sir Gawain exclaimed, looking sharply at Terence. "Is that where Lancelot's been since he left the court? Cutting wood?"

Terence nodded. "I told him I'd keep it quiet, so don't go spreading it about. Either of you."

Piers could only stare. Sir Lancelot! Even in the isolation of his father's blacksmith shop, Piers had heard how Sir Lancelot had gone mad and disappeared from the court after being shamed by some sorcerer. Had Piers really lived for three months alongside the most famous of all knights without knowing it?

Terence cleared his throat. "I believe Lancelot has decided that knightly pursuits, or at least his own understanding of them, were sort of pointless. But I'm glad to hear he hasn't given up his skills entirely. Your master, Piers, seems to have fallen in with at least one good teacher."

*

Piers rode the next few miles in silence, still awestruck over his discovery that Jean was Sir Lancelot. Terence and Sir Gawain continued to talk, but after a while they stopped and leaned forward, listening. "Your ears are better than mine, Terence," Sir Gawain said. "A full cohort?"

"Not quite so much. Two hundred horses, but they have at least one wagon. Planning a siege perhaps."

Piers strained his ears and at last heard what the others had noted: a muted rumble in the distance.

"Let's go see," Sir Gawain said.

There was no talking as they rode now. In a minute, Piers could see a low cloud of dust rising over an irregular band of trees ahead. They rode right into the grove, then walked their horses slowly through it and looked out the other side. There, flashing and glinting and rumbling in the dust and sun, was an army on the move, much larger than either of King Clamide's forces had been. Terence made a motion to Sir Gawain, who nodded, and then Terence rode his horse out of the trees and joined the procession.

Gawain glanced at Piers's mystified look and explained. "He's going to find out what's going on. People always talk to Terence."

Sure enough, in a few minutes Terence reappeared, followed by another young man in squire's clothes. "Milord," Terence said, grinning, "allow me to introduce Squire Brevard. I thought I'd let him tell the tale himself."

Squire Brevard looked closely at Sir Gawain. "I didn't half believe your squire," he said, "but I guess you might be Sir Gawain, after all."

"I am relieved to hear you say so," Sir Gawain replied solemnly. "I confess that I've always thought so myself."

Squire Brevard chuckled, but then grew serious again. "I've heard it said that you understand love."

"No one understands love," Sir Gawain said. "But understanding is much overvalued. Perhaps I can help you, anyway. Are you in love?"

"It's not me; it's my master, Sir Malchance."

Sir Gawain smiled. "What an unfortunate name," he murmured. Piers hid a grin. *Malchance* was French for "bad luck".

"It's not his name that's unfortunate," Brevard said bitterly. "It's his temper."

"Tell me the story," Sir Gawain said.

"All right, although it's no pleasure to tell. My master, Sir Malchance, is the son of King Lys, but the king died when Malchance was a child and, according to his father's dying request, Malchance was taken to Duke Lyppaut to raise as his own. Now this Lyppaut has two daughters, and the eldest, Lady Obie, is the fairest lady in the land."

Brevard made this last comment in the lofty tones of a minstrel. Sir Gawain chuckled. "I'll bet."

Brevard grinned back. "Actually, she's not so bad looking. Her younger sister Obilot is prettier, though. Anyway, Malchance grew up, studied knighthood, was knighted by Lyppaut himself, and of course fell in love with Obie."

"Of course," Sir Gawain said.

"So he proposed marriage, and she turned him down."

"Didn't care for him, eh?"

Brevard shook his head decidedly. "No, that's the silly part of it. Obie's as much in love in Malchance as he is with her. I know. I used to deliver their secret love letters."

"Secret? Why secret? Surely this Lyppaut doesn't disapprove?"

Brevard laughed. "Their marriage is his fondest dream. But Obie's of a rather – ah – romantical disposition."

"I see," Sir Gawain said, shaking his head sadly. "She thought it would be romantic to have a secret love – private meetings, messages in code, secret signals at dinner . . . "

Brevard nodded. "All of that and more."

"So why did she turn him down?" Gawain asked.

"Another romantical notion," Brevard said disgustedly. "She dreams of a valiant knight, and so she said that until Malchance had proven himself in battle, she could never marry him. So, in a black rage, he went off and raised an army, and now we're about to lay siege to Lyppaut's castle to demand that he let Obie marry him."

"Thus forcing Lyppaut to do what he's always wanted to do anyway," Sir Gawain said, laughing suddenly.

"Milord?" Terence said. "I know you're the Maiden's Knight and all that, but I don't suppose you could give this one a miss, could you?" Sir Gawain laughed again, and Terence muttered, "I didn't think so."

It was no trouble at all for Sir Gawain and his companions to join the ranks without notice. Sir Malchance had hired his soldiers from all over England, and few knew any of the others. Piers was dazzled by the array of arms and armour about him, but Sir Gawain and Terence regarded most of the other knights with amusement. When he asked

Terence why, Terence replied, "I doubt if more than half of these fellows have ever been in armour in their lives. This Malchance probably offered to pay his knights a year's wages and every squire and manservant and ploughboy who could find a suit of arms joined up for a lark." His smile faded. "I hope no one is hurt in this folly."

The next day they arrived at Duke Lyppaut's home, a squat, modest sort of castle, set in a broad, flat plain. They rode close, and as soon as they were within ear-shot of the walls, a man in silver armour rode out of the vanguard and raised his lance in the air. "Come to me, all my captains!" he shouted.

Sir Gawain, sitting on his huge black horse beside Piers, chuckled. "What do you want to bet that Malchance doesn't even know who his hired captains are?" He clicked his tongue and his horse trotted forward and joined the group. A few of the other knights looked at him curiously, but no one said a word. Malchance rode a few steps forward, his captains and Sir Gawain at his heels, and called out. "Duke Lyppaut! Thou traitor! Show thyself!"

A white-haired man looked over the battlements. Piers could see two female figures beside him. "What is it, son?" the duke asked mildly.

"I have come to demand of thee what is truly mine."

Duke Lyppaut shrugged. "Everything I have is yours. You know that."

This threw Malchance out of his rhythm, and he hesitated. Piers almost felt sorry for him. It must be hard to sound threatening when your victim calls you "son" and willingly offers you whatever you want. At last he recovered. "I have not yet told you what I demand, sirrah! I have come to take your eldest daughter from you, whatsoever say ye!"

Duke Lyppaut's face lit with a joyous smile. "In truth? Oh, Malchance, if only her mother were here to see—"

"Tell him he wastes his time!" shouted a voice beside the duke. It was one of the ladies. "Tell him that I shall have none of him." The duke clearly was surprised. He said something in an undervoice to his daughter, but she only tossed her head and declared, "Never! Should I, the daughter of a duke, marry myself to a beardless, untried youth?"

"His beard will come in soon enough," the duke said placatingly. "I thought you liked—"

"Like this child? I laugh at the idea." Then, as if to prove her words, the lady added a grim, "Ha-ha!"

Malchance uttered an oath and then shouted

furiously, "Then I shall fight! And when I have slain every one of your knights, then perhaps you shall think differently, my Lady Scorn!"

Duke Lyppaut turned abruptly and shouted across his own castle walls. "Listen to me, men! Not one of you will take up arms against Malchance. Do you understand me? No fighting Malchance!"

"What?" Malchance demanded, beside himself. "You can't do that!"

"I won't have my future son-in-law hurt!" the duke shouted back.

"He's not your future son-in-law!" the lady declared. "I won't marry him, I tell you!" She put her hand on her forehead and looked over her shoulder at her father's knights. "Oh, will none of you champion me against this my oppressor?"

"No, they won't, and that's that," Duke Lyppaut snapped. "Look here, Obie, have you and Chance had a quarrel?"

Malchance interrupted, shouting again, "You can't do that, Uncle Lyppaut! I've come to fight, I tell you! I will prove my honour in battle, before your very eyes!"

"Not with my men, you won't," the duke said abruptly.

Lady Obie raised her eyes to the sky and cried

out, "Then may the gods themselves send me a defender!"

"I'll fight him for you," said a pleasant voice. It was Sir Gawain.

"You?" Malchance demanded. "But you're one of my own men."

"No, I'm not. I just joined up for the ride. Lady Obie? I'll fight Malchance for you, if you like."

Lady Obie hesitated, then turned her nose up in the air. "No," she said at last. "I don't like you. You look like a fishmonger."

Sir Gawain laughed easily. "Despite my appearance, though, I really am a knight, and I'll happily bash your boy if you like."

"Well, I don't," Obie snapped. "So go away!"

Piers shook his head in bewilderment. Terence, sitting beside him, said softly, "Curious, isn't it? People make love so complicated for themselves."

Now a new player joined the discussion, the other lady who was standing beside Duke Lyppaut. "Sir knight?" she called down to Sir Gawain. "Will you really fight Malchance?"

"I already told him no, Obilot," Obie interjected. "He can't fight my battles if I don't want him to. It's in the code of chivalry."

"I'm here, too, you know," the lady replied. As she stepped up to the battlements, Piers saw that she was very young. "Sir knight, would you fight Malchance for me instead of for my sister?"

Sir Gawain chuckled. "It would be an honour, my lady. Just say the word."

"All right then," the young lady said. "Go to it."

Sir Gawain reached over and pushed Malchance off his horse. Malchance scrambled out of the dust, spluttering with fury. "Don't just stand there, you fools! Get him!"

"Here we go," Terence muttered, drawing a long sword from his saddle and spurring his horse ahead to join his master. Unarmed but of no mind to be left behind, Piers followed at a gallop and took a place with his back to the castle walls. In a moment, Sir Gawain and Terence were both laying about with their swords, driving Malchance's unprepared captains back toward the rest of the army. Malchance himself, being on foot, had already scurried back to the lines, out of the way of the stomping horses. Then one of the captains raised his hands in the air in a signal for a halt. Sir Gawain and Terence stopped, but held their swords ready.

The knight who had called the halt leaned forward in the saddle. "Is that you, Terence?"

Terence cocked his head. "My name *is* Terence," he replied.

The knight opened the visor on his helm and showed a smiling face. "Well, how've you been, old man? It's me, Astor!"

"By Avalon!" Terence exclaimed. "How are you, friend? Did your master knight you already?" Terence glanced at Sir Gawain. "Astor used to be Sagramore's squire."

"Look here, Terence," Astor said. "You've got us on the run right now, but you know we outnumber you a hundred to one. Even with these clodpoles and dirt farmers we've got, you're going to be in trouble soon."

"Yes, that's true," Terence said. "But I don't see what to do about it."

Astor smiled. "Well, I was thinking of joining your side. I've no taste for fighting someone else's family quarrel. I've got a dozen men with me, skilled knights all. It should make for a good turn up, don't you think?"

Terence smiled. "What do you say, milord? Shall we?"

Sir Gawain nodded and handed Terence his shield. "Here, lad, don't take any chances. You've no armour on, after all. Well, fellows – charge!"

And then the battle began. Piers, watching from the castle wall, could see little of what was going on. Occasionally he caught a glimpse of Sir

Gawain's mountainous black horse, but he was not a very skilled observer of knightly combat, and most of the time he couldn't tell who was fighting whom. A few of the knights from inside the castle opened the castle gates and strolled out to watch. One was munching on some bread and cheese.

"You know, lads," the knight said between bites. "This is the best siege I've ever been part of."

"Hear, hear," the others replied. A few of them stretched out in the grass, so as to more comfortably watch their would-be besiegers fight each other.

Above Piers's head, on the wall, a female voice said, "I think my fishmonger has just knocked your betrothed off his horse again."

"He's not my betrothed, and you just shut up! This is all your fault, Obilot!" Lady Obie retorted.

"*My* fault! Well of all the poisonous cats! *I'm* not the one who sent Malchance off with a beetle in his bottom. If you ask me, you don't know what you want, sister."

Lady Obie responded by bursting into tears.

The fight in the meadow seemed to be less confusing than it had been a few minutes before, and Piers realized that Malchance's "knights" were sneaking off and riding away in groups of two and three. Before the battle had gone half an hour, there were only a score of knights left on their feet, and most of those were the knights with Sir Gawain. Piers saw Malchance approach Sir Gawain, waving his sword. Sir Gawain nodded and dismounted, and the other knights backed away. Evidently they had decided to settle matters with single combat.

"I hope my fishmonger doesn't get hurt," young Obilot commented.

"Shut up, I tell you!" Obie snapped.

"Sir knight!" called Duke Lyppaut from the wall. "I'll give you a hundredweight of Roman gold if you promise not to hurt Malchance!"

Then the two knights fought. Even to Piers it was clear that Sir Gawain was never in any danger, although Malchance certainly attacked with great vigour. At last, Sir Gawain knocked Malchance to the ground, stepped on his sword, and then pointed his own sword at Malchance's throat. Malchance yielded.

All the knights walked slowly back across the field toward the castle, just as Duke Lyppaut and his daughters stepped out of the gates. Malchance, who had led the way, fell to his knees before Lady Obie. "You were right, Obie. I'm only a child. I'm not worthy of you."

"Oh, I wouldn't say that," Sir Gawain said

bracingly. "You fought well out there, and most important, you kept getting back up when I knocked you down. Best thing you could do."

"But you should never have knocked me down to start with."

"Oh, there's no shame in that. Everyone can take a fall. Even those of us from the Round Table."

Malchance looked up. "You're with the Round Table?" he asked.

"That's right. My name's Gawain."

In the hush that followed, only one voice spoke. "I suppose that means you're not a fishmonger, doesn't it?" said Obilot.

Sir Gawain grinned, but turned his attention to Malchance. "So you see, you fought a famous knight, and you did well. I think you've proven yourself now. Perhaps the Lady Obie will consent to your request now."

Then, to everyone's surprise, Duke Lyppaut interrupted. "No, I say! She can't marry him!"

"What?" asked a dozen voices at once.

"How can I give my daughter to the man who attacked her family? No, no. It is impossible." Duke Lyppaut turned an ingratiating smile on Sir Gawain and continued. "It is much more fitting that she should marry her rescuer. Sir Gawain, I believe I've never heard that you were married."

Piers looked sharply at Sir Gawain, who was passing his hand over his eyes. Terence moaned softly, and Malchance and Obie looked at each other, aghast.

"No!" said young Obilot suddenly. "He can't marry Obie. After all, he fought for me. If he is to marry anyone, it should be me!" Now everyone turned their astonishment toward Obilot, but Piers did not miss the quick wink that Obilot gave to Sir Gawain.

Sir Gawain chuckled and knelt at Obilot's feet. "As you wish, my lady," he said.

"Wait just a minute, here!" came a new voice. It was the squire that Terence had met on the trail, Brevard. "You can't marry him, Obilot!"

"Why not, Brevard?" she asked.

"Well, you're ... you're too young. And you might still meet someone you like more."

"Like who, Brevard?" Obilot said demurely.

"Well ... like me."

Obilot smiled at Sir Gawain and shrugged. "Sorry, Sir Gawain," she said.

Piers was growing more and more confused, and from the faces around him he was sure that others felt the same way. Fortunately, at that moment, Obilot stepped into the centre of the circle of onlookers and raised her hand. "All right, now, let's finish this. Father, you are ambitious and silly. Sir Gawain doesn't want to marry either of us, and so he shan't. Malchance and Obie, you are very boring, always fighting in public. I wish you would just go get married so you could fight in private. And as for you, Brevard, we shall talk of this further." And with a wave of her diminutive hand she dismissed the crowd.

Rising to his feet, Sir Gawain bowed and kissed Obilot's hand. "My lady, it has been a great pleasure, a very great pleasure, to meet you. Keep them in hand, will you?"

Then he mounted his black horse, turned his head back toward the woods, and he and Terence and Piers rode away. "Milord?" Terence said, as they crested a hill.

"Yes, lad?"

"Let's try to the northwest."

"Why?"

"I was just talking with Astor. He says that there's a red knight in Wales who's been winning all sorts of battles."

7

QUESTING

They rode toward Wales, leaving the fields and plains and then climbing wooded hills. Piers was still often startled by the casual manners that Sir Gawain and his squire used with each other, as if they were equals, but as time went on he began to lapse into the same familiar manner. At the knight's insistence, Piers even stopped using the full title *Sir* Gawain, and began calling him simply Gawain.

It would have been hard to stay too formal, anyway, given the division of duties in their camps. Everyone pitched in and did part of the work, and no task was considered below anyone. Terence did all the hunting and cooking, and Gawain cleaned and oiled his own armour – a squire's task if there ever was one. After the first day, Piers took over caring for the horses. Gawain's black horse sometimes snapped at him and always watched Piers suspiciously, but Piers was used to fidgety horses. He had often held horses while his father shod them.

"You seem to be good with horses, Piers," Gawain commented. "Guingalet there doesn't usually let strangers curry him."

Piers was pleased, but said only, "I've never been afraid of horses."

"Nothing wrong with being afraid of Guingalet," Terence remarked. "He's half devil. He's a bit calmer these days, but when he was young, no one could get close to him but Gawain."

"Shush," Gawain said. "You'll hurt his feelings." He glanced fondly at his horse. "Don't listen to him, old fellow. I know you're as nasty as ever."

They rode into the Welsh hills, still heading north, meeting no one that they could ask about a red knight. On the third day, though, Piers felt a growing excitement. The woods around him looked the same as always, but now he had an odd sense of expectation. At mid-afternoon they came upon a castle in the woods. Gawain drew up at the edge of the forest. "What do you think, Terence?"

"I don't know, milord. Have you been feeling it, too?"

"Ay, something not natural in the air."

"Not bad, though," Terence added. "Just...
uncanny. Why don't you and Piers go and ask after
the red knight, while I scout around outside?"

Gawain nodded, and Terence slipped
soundlessly from his saddle and seemed to melt
into the forest. "Come on, Piers," Gawain said.

They rode into the cleared area before the castle,
where a trail of smoke rose from a sturdy stone
cottage outside the gates. As they drew near, a
rough-looking man stepped out and raised his
hand in silent greeting.

"Hello," Sir Gawain called. "Is this castle
inhabited?"

"Ay," the man said. "What do you want?"
Gawain raised his eyebrows, and the man smiled
ruefully. "Didn't mean to be rude. We get few
visitors. My name's Waleis, and I'm the reeve here
– and chief gamekeeper and steward, and if the
master were a bit more grand, I'd be called the
seneschal, too. If you need anything, you may as
well ask me first, because you'll get sent back out
to me anyway."

Gawain nodded. "We're looking for a red knight
that we've heard has been in these parts. Have you
any word of him?"

Waleis shook his head. "Nay. You're the first

outsider to stop here in near six months."

"I see," Gawain said. "Then perhaps, since the day is closing, your master would allow us to stay the night in his castle. It would be pleasant to sleep in a bed again."

Waleis nodded. "No harm in that. And the mistress will be glad of the company." Waleis bit his lip and frowned, as if he had more to say, and Gawain waited. Waleis said, "I suppose I'd best just tell you. The master's a bit odd. Never quite got over the old master's death – his father, you know. Keeps to himself mostly."

"Oh? If it would be better for us not to stay —"

"Nay, that's not what I meant. I only wanted to warn you that you may see the master and you may not. In any case, his sister will make you welcome. You'll come to no harm inside."

Gawain nodded. "Thank you, friend. My squire is on the trail behind us and may come up at any time. If he arrives, would you send him in please?"

Waleis acknowledged Gawain's request with a careless wave and then went back inside his cottage. Gawain and Piers rode through the open castle gates into the courtyard.

Two ladies stood in the courtyard, washing clothes in a large tub and talking, but when they saw Gawain they dropped everything and ran with a shriek into the castle keep. "What do you think's wrong with them?" Gawain asked. "Usually kitchen maids aren't so excitable."

"They weren't kitchen maids," Piers said confidently. "Their gowns were too fine. Those were ladies-in-waiting." Gawain looked at Piers with amusement, and Piers explained, "My mother was a lady-in-waiting, too. Those ladies probably ran inside because they didn't want a knight to see them doing menial work."

Gawain pursed his lips thoughtfully. "I see. The reeve did say they weren't used to company. So now I suppose they'll braid each other's hair and sprinkle themselves with eau de toilette before coming out again. Shall we put up the horses while we wait?" Piers grinned and nodded.

Forty minutes later, their horses long since stabled and fed, the mistress of the castle came sweeping into the yard, dressed in a dazzling red gown. "Sir knight!" the lady trilled. "I am so sorry that you had to wait! My foolish women only just now told me that a knight had come to call, and I threw down my stitchery and came at once!" Piers rolled his eyes, but discreetly. As if anyone ever wore such a gown for a quiet day at home doing needlework.

"It is of no matter," Gawain said, bowing

graciously. "To see such beauty would well reward even a much longer wait."

The lady blushed and tittered and said that she could see she'd have to watch herself with such a wickedly gallant knight and some other stuff like that. She introduced herself as the Lady Antigone, and then paused, clearly waiting for Gawain to give his name in return, but Gawain only bowed again, said that he was enchanted, and asked if her name was Greek.

"Why, yes, it is! Fancy you recognizing that! I don't think I've ever known anyone else who knew that. I don't know what it means, of course, but my father named all his children after people in old books."

"Ah, a learned man, then?"

Lady Antigone hesitated, then nodded. "Well, yes, I suppose you would say that, but really you mustn't think ill of him. Why, he was so handsome and brave that no one would ever have suspected that he was bookish!"

Gawain continued smiling, but his smile seemed forced now. "You mistake me, my lady. I meant no disrespect. I understand that even King Arthur reads Greek."

Lady Antigone's lips parted in surprise. "You don't say! Well, it only goes to show that even the great ones have their peculiarities."

"Quite so," replied Gawain, sighing softly.

"Well, you'll find better entertainment in this house, I can assure you! Why, we'll have a great banquet tonight! Matilde, Gwen, show this knight and his boy with the charming hat to the best bed chambers to dress for dinner!"

And so, a few minutes later, Piers and Gawain found themselves alone in a well-furnished but dusty bedroom. "Whew!" Gawain said. "No wonder they have few visitors here. What a gabblemonger! I suppose it's too late to slip out the back way."

Piers took off his scarlet hat, frowning slightly. Gawain and Terence wore such plain, simple clothes on the trail that Piers had begun to feel self-conscious about his bright headwear. To have the hat complimented by the overdressed Lady Antigone had only increased his doubts. He helped Gawain remove his armour.

"I wonder what I should do with my sword," Gawain mused. "I never know, when I'm dining at a stranger's home, if I should wear it to dinner as a precaution or trust in the laws of hospitality."

Piers did not reply. Two weeks ago, with Parsifal, he was full of advice, most of it wrong. This time he would venture no opinion. At last Gawain threw the sword on the bed. "I suppose I'm in no danger from Lady Prattles."

But when they at last went to dine with Lady Antigone, Piers was not so sure. There was more than one kind of danger after all, and Antigone was surely setting her own sort of traps for Gawain. The "great banquet" that she had promised turned out to be a cosy dinner for two in a candlelit parlour. There were two long chaises at the table, one on each side, but when Gawain sat in one, Lady Antigone joined him, sitting almost in his lap. As soon as the meal had been served, she dismissed her two ladies-in-waiting and suggested that Gawain could send his boy away, too.

"Oh, I couldn't," Gawain replied promptly. "Piers is so useful that I would be lost without him. In fact, step closer, Piers."

Piers came nearer, while Lady Antigone pursed her lips pettishly. "May I serve your plate, sir knight? You know, it really is silly of me to keep saying 'sir knight'. What is your name?"

"What is a name anyway, my lady?" Gawain replied, edging away from her. "It is only a monument to one's ancestors. I prefer to be known by my deeds than by my name."

"Oh!" Lady Antigone purred. "A man of action."

Gawain stood abruptly and walked around the room. "Very nice parlour this is," he said.

"It is very comfortable, Sir Man of Action, but you do not appear to be relaxed. Come sit beside me and I will give you a morsel of food."

"I'm not all that hungry after all," Gawain said. "How about...how about a game of chess?" He strode across the room to an old chess table by the window. The chessmen were large and looked heavy.

"That was my father's game," Lady Antigone said. "He tried to teach me, but I never liked it."

"Of course not," Gawain said resignedly. He walked back to the table, sitting on the chaise across from his hostess. "Would you...would you like some chicken?"

"Oh, sir knight," Lady Antigone said, lifting her chin to show off a very white throat, "I can't tell you how long I have waited for such a moment as this!"

"I can see why," Gawain said, taking a bite. "This chicken's excellent. Really, I must congratulate your cook. How does he get it so tender?"

"Oh, hang the chicken!"

"Is that how it's done?" Gawain asked. "I must tell my own cook to try that."

"I'm not talking about the chicken!" Lady Antigone exclaimed. "I'm talking about you and I!"

"You and *me*," Gawain said. "Not you and *I*. Use the accusative case."

"I do not want to accuse you, O knight. I want to love you." She started around the table.

"Ah, then you'll want the optative, I think," Gawain replied, starting around the table the other way. "But I was never good at that one."

"Sir knight!" she said dramatically. "I love you! Kiss me!"

Gawain never had to reply, for at that moment a fully armed knight burst into the room waving a sword. "Has it come to this?" the knight bellowed. "Was it not enough that you killed my father, but now you must seduce my sister!"

"Virgil!" Lady Antigone shrieked. "What are you doing?"

"I have come for to slay this knight, for he is the man who slew my noble father Sir Kingrisin!"

"Daddy died of the ague!" Lady Antigone said.

"Nay, but this man is the murderer! Stand and fight!"

Gawain had moved to keep the table between him and the knight and now he spoke. "As you see, my friend, I am unarmed."

"So too was my father when he died!" the knight exclaimed.

"He's right, there," admitted Lady Antigone, nodding as if her brother had made a good point. "Daddy died in bed, you see."

"I am sorry that your father died," Gawain said steadily. "But I did not kill him. Nor have I seduced your sister."

Lady Antigone stepped in front of her brother and said, "There, see? Now be good and leave us alone."

"That shall I not, thou strumpet!" the knight shouted. He tried to push his sister out of his way, but she clung to his armoured arm.

"Please, Virgil! I hate this place! I hate living here all alone with no visitors! Please don't ruin everything!" The knight, Sir Virgil, tried to shake his sister off, but she only clung more tightly to his arm, and for the next several moments the night was filled with the shouting of the brother and shrieking of the sister. Gawain kept the table between himself and the fray.

Piers, ignored by the others, had slipped into the shadows by the window and now began to look desperately about for some weapon he could give Gawain. There was nothing. Then his eyes fell on the chessboard beside him, and he lifted one of the rooks. It was even heavier than he'd expected. Solid lead, he decided, weighing it in his hand. He took up the heaviest one he could find. The white king.

"This murderer has bewitched you, woman!" shouted the knight, in a frenzy. "And for that he must die!"

He swung his sword down on the table, which split into two halves, sending chicken fragments flying. The knight stepped over the rubble toward Gawain, and Piers threw the white king with all his might. It was a good shot, right at eye level, and might have even dented the knight's helm had it not bounced instead off of the Lady Antigone's forehead. She stopped screaming, made a sound sort of like "Gloop", and sat down heavily on the floor amid the splinters and bits of chicken.

"Sorry," Piers said. Lady Antigone closed her eyes and lay down peacefully.

"King to Queen Two," Gawain said.

The knight, who had stopped his advance momentarily, looked up from his sister's prone form and raised his sword again. Piers began grabbing more men from the table and throwing them as fast as he could. Most missed, but a black bishop hit the knight full in the visor, and several pawns bounced off his armour. Gawain leaped backwards toward Piers and swept up the whole chess table in his hand, holding it like a shield. "Stay behind me," he hissed to Piers.

The knight charged, and Gawain parried the flashing sword with the table. A deep chip flew from the edge, but the table held. Again the knight attacked, and again Gawain warded off the blow, leaving the chessboard nicked a second time. "Piers," Gawain hissed. "See if there's a door behind that arras."

Piers nodded and ducked across the room. Behind him he heard the sound of another sword blow on the table, but he did not look back. He tore at the long, hanging drapes, which ripped entirely from their hangings and collapsed in a dust cloud at Piers's feet. There was no door behind it. Piers whirled about, still holding one end of the arras in his hand and saw Gawain deflect another sword stroke with his chess table shield.

"Get away while you can, Piers!" Gawain shouted, gesturing to the door they had come in, but Piers only looked about for something else to throw at the knight. Then Sir Virgil swung a mighty blow down onto the table shield and split it in two. Without hesitating, Gawain shifted his grip to the largest half and swung it like a club into his foe. Sir Virgil took a quick step backwards, and

Piers threw the arras over his head. Gawain, seeing Sir Virgil blinded by the drape, threw himself against the knight and knocked him sprawling on the floor.

Then the door burst open, and Waleis the Reeve entered, brandishing his own sword. "What's going on, Virgil?"

"This...this knight killed father," the knight said hoarsely, through the folds of the arras.

"No, he didn't," Waleis snapped. The reeve stooped over his master and whipped the drape from his face. "Put that sword down at once! I promised this knight that he'd be safe here."

"I have to avenge father," the knight said brokenly, sitting up.

Waleis spoke in a milder tone, but still firmly. "Your father just died, Virgil. It's not this knight's fault, not your fault, not anybody's fault. Leave this knight alone."

Sir Virgil lowered his sword, then bowed his head and began to cry. Waleis jerked his head toward the door and said to Gawain, "I'll stay with him now. There's not much of him left, but we were boys together, and he's still my master."

Gawain nodded. He set down the split table and led Piers out the door and back down the hall to their bedchamber. Neither spoke until they had closed the door behind them, and then Gawain said softly, "Poor Sir Virgil." He looked briefly at Piers. "You did well in there, Piers. Very well indeed. Pawn takes knight."

Piers carried those words with him to sleep.

The next morning they took their leave of the gruff Waleis and the very glum Lady Antigone, who was sporting a terrific goose egg on her brow, and rode into the forest, where Terence was waiting for them. "I hope you've had a pleasant evening, Terence," Gawain said acidly.

"Why, yes, thank you," said Terence. "And you?"

"Splendid," Gawain muttered. "Very restful."

Terence glanced knowingly at his friend. "Whatever happened, you don't seem any the worse for wear."

Gawain snorted and favoured Terence with a pithy account of the previous evening's goings-on. When the tale was done, Terence nodded approvingly at Piers. Gawain concluded his story, saying, "I suppose Sir Virgil is too fragile for the grief of this world."

"Grief is not confined to this world," Terence said.

"But enough of our story," Gawain said. "What

have you been doing? Did you ever find where that uncanny feeling was coming from?"

Terence shook his head, but his face was calm. "No. We're being followed by someone from the Seelie Court, but whoever it is wasn't looking for me. I met no one, and by the time I gave up, it was late so I simply made camp in the woods." When Terence mentioned the Seelie Court, Piers jumped and glanced quickly around them at the forest. All was still and calm. Terence continued. "Now I wonder why it is," he said musingly, "that our young companion did not ask me to explain what the Seelie Court is. Do you suppose he already knows, milord?"

Gawain grinned, but said nothing. Piers looked down, feeling almost guilty for not telling his friends about his encounter with the little sprite Ariel, but it was too private. After a moment, Terence looked at Gawain and said, "What about the quest, milord? Did you get any word of this elusive red knight?"

"No."

For the rest of the morning, they rode through forests so thick that they had to travel single-file. Piers purposely took the last position so that he could look about him unobtrusively for some sign of an Other Worldly messenger. He saw nothing, but the same sense of anticipation that he had felt the day before began to grow. At noon they stopped for a short rest and a meal, and while Piers built a fire Gawain and Terence disappeared into the woods.

"Piers!"

Piers jumped and whirled around. There, in the underbrush, was Ariel. Piers smiled joyously and hurried into the woods beside her. She greeted him with a smile and held out her hand. Piers did not hesitate, but grasped it, noting with interest that her hand was as warm and solid as his own. He'd never thought about how a faery might feel. "Hello, Ariel," Piers said.

Ariel blushed. "I wasn't sure you'd remember my name," she said.

Piers could only stare at her – as if he'd ever gone an hour without wondering about her! For some reason that he could not quite put into words, he knew that he would never like or trust anyone else the way he did this little faery. It wasn't love – at least, it was nothing like the silly mixture of attraction and competition that he had seen in Malchance and Obie, and nothing at all like the repugnant hot and cold emotion that existed between Duke Orilus and Lady Jeschute – it was just that he liked her. "Of course I remember your name. I remember everything that you told me. Although," he added, "that's not saying much."

Ariel smiled and sat on a mossy log, spreading her simple white shift over her lap with her free hand. Piers sat beside her. "What would you like to know?" she asked.

"Everything."

Ariel giggled. "I don't have time for everything. Besides, most of everything is boring. Let me see. My name is Ariel, and my mother is named Nimue. She's the most beautiful creature in any world. My father is named Myrddin. As for the rest, I've had a terribly dull life. Mother never even let me visit this world until just recently. I had found the mouth of the cave by myself, you know, by the waterfall, and I thought it wouldn't hurt anything to just go out and take a look. I knew I was safe as long as I stayed in the water. That's when you appeared and scared me to death."

"Sorry."

"I was so afraid that I'd done something terrible, but when I told Mother, she said that now I was old enough, and that's when she let me go back to give you those instructions."

"'Follow the water,'" Piers said. He realized guiltily that he hadn't thought about the instructions since that night. He'd been too busy thinking about Ariel. "What did those instructions mean?"

Ariel shrugged. "I was hoping *you* would know. Mother says you have the look of someone from a great family."

"But I'm not," Piers said. "My father is a blacksmith, and my mother is a retired lady-in-waiting. I'm from about as un-great a family as you can be from."

"Mother's usually right about these things," Ariel said doubtfully. "But I can ask her again."

There was a rustling in the brush not far away, and Ariel jumped. "Oh! No one but you is supposed to see me!"

"Then it *was* you following us yesterday and this morning!" Piers whispered. "I was almost sure it was. Did you have to hide from Terence?"

"Is that the squire who came looking for me?" Ariel asked. Piers nodded. "Yes, although I hated to do it. He looked half like he was from the Seelie Court himself." There was another rustling, and Piers heard Gawain's voice. "Quickly!" Ariel whispered. "You're to go due north, along the coast toward Scotland, to a hermit's cottage. The man you're looking for is there." Ariel gave Piers's hand a gentle squeeze, and then slipped away. Piers watched until she came to a small brook, and then she disappeared, like mist.

When Piers stepped out of the underbrush into the camp, Terence and Gawain were sprawled comfortably beneath a tree. "Well?" Terence said. "Did your friend tell us which way to go?"

Piers gave a tiny nod. "North," he said, and neither Gawain nor Terence asked anything more.

Three days later, as they rode through a peaceful, airy wood, Terence pulled up suddenly.

"What is it, lad?" asked Gawain.

"Now I know where we are," Terence said abruptly. "This has been looking familiar for over an hour. We're in the Gentle Wood, where Trevisant's hermitage is."

"Hermitage?" Piers demanded suddenly. "But that's it! That's where we're to go! Ar— my friend said to go to a hermit's cottage."

Terence grinned broadly. "Just follow me!" he said, kicking his horse into a gallop.

Half an hour later they pulled up in a dusty yard outside a small stone house. An ancient man was dipping water from a well, but he walked unsteadily over to greet the visitors.

"Trevisant!" Terence shouted joyfully. He threw himself from his saddle and ran across the yard to embrace the man. Trevisant returned Terence's embrace, then held the squire at arm's length and looked into his face.

"Now let me see," the hermit said. "Do I know you?"

Terence's smile disappeared, and he looked stricken. Then the squire took a sharp breath, and his chin dropped onto his chest. "Of course," Terence said. "I never thought of that."

"What is, lad?" Gawain asked.

"You remember Trevisant's peculiarity, don't you, milord? That he sees the past the way we see the future and the future the way we see the past."

"I see," Gawain said. "You mean that he doesn't remember you."

"Or else has never met me," Terence said softly.

Trevisant inclined his head. "I must indeed know you," he said. "For you certainly know me."

"I do know you, sir. I grew up here. You raised me from the time I was a baby until I was a youth. You were father to me."

The old man touched Terence's cheek with one gnarled finger. "And I don't remember you. I am so sorry, my son."

Terence's face contorted, but his voice was steady. "It doesn't matter. I would care for you if you remembered nothing at all."

Trevisant smiled brightly. "What a lovely thing

to say. I must have raised you well."

They all laughed, although it was a strained sort of laugh, and the old man burst into a fit of coughing that actually doubled him over. Terence supported him while he coughed, and when the paroxysm had passed, led him to a bench in the sun.

"That did not sound very good, sir," Terence said. "Have you been coughing like that for long?"

Trevisant smiled again. "It is funny that you should have just now said something about my remembering nothing at all. Because the time is soon when that will be true."

"Are you . . . are you sure?" Terence asked quickly. Trevisant only smiled, and Terence nodded. "Of course you're sure."

The old man laid one hand on Terence's arm. "Please don't distress yourself. Remember, I've always known how it would end with me. It will be soon, and it will be peaceful. I have just completed my final task."

Gawain, who had dismounted, stood before Trevisant, holding Guingalet's reins. "What task was that, sir?" It struck Piers that in all their days together, he could not remember that Gawain had called anyone "sir" until now.

"I have shown my book to Parsifal," the old man said.

Terence and Gawain and Piers all looked at each other. At last Gawain asked, "Is Parsifal still here?"

"Oh, no. He left...I'm not sure. It may have been this morning, or perhaps yesterday morning. If it had been longer ago than that, I would have forgotten."

"Where has he gone?" Gawain asked.

"I do not know. My book might tell you. Perhaps you, son, would go inside and get it. It will answer many questions, I hope."

Terence went inside. Piers could hear him moving things around. After a minute, he reappeared in the doorway holding a heavy book with thick vellum pages. "I never saw this book, in all the years I lived with you," Terence commented. "I wonder where you had it hidden."

"Well, you can't expect me to know," Trevisant said. "Read it."

Terence opened the book and read.

"My name is called Sir Trevisant, Knight Templar of the Schloss Munsalvaesche, prince of the blood, brother to the noblest of all kings, the good King Anfortas, who unto this day livest in torment, and whose land be laid waste in mourning for his grief.

"I write my name because I know not if in the days

to come I shall remember even that, for what hath come unto me is like unto what hath come upon no other mortal. My birth, my childhood, all are slipping from me, and though I need them not in my new life, I must not forget what hath brought me to this place in the Gentle Wood.

"My brother Anfortas is king over Munsalvaesche, at the very navel of two worlds, a door between the World of Men and the World of Faeries that shall not close until that time when every such door is closed. On a day not so very long ago, Anfortas rode alone into the woods and met a lone knight. This knight was very like unto Anfortas, the same in every feature and every manner of speech, save that his face was dark and his hair white, the same and yet the opposite. The lone knight challenged Anfortas in such churlish fashion that Anfortas was wonderly amazed, and he did take up the challenge and thus brought upon himself and all the land great misery.

"For the knight gave Anfortas a grievous wound, leaving him nigh unto death, but then a good enchanter named Ganscotter came unto the castle and gave our assembly a great magic which is called the Grail, and whenever Anfortas sets eyes on this Grail, his life is preserved for yet another time. Before he left, the enchanter said that only the One Who Had Been Chosen might heal the king.

157

"I was a young knight then, and proud. I did not believe the enchanter's words and rode after the knight who had wounded my brother to fight him. I found him and was able to take his lance from him, but I could not overcome him. I returned to Munsalvaesche with the lance, swearing that some day I should heal my brother and restore the land.

"To this end I and my sister Herzeloyde and a faithful servant, the great armourer Trebuchet, set out together to find this One Who Had Been Chosen. I will not repeat all of our trials, for they were greater and more grievous than I care to remember, and I am relieved that soon I shall be spared those memories forever. My sister left our quest first, for she was weary of the endless barren search, and married a knight of Anjou. Then I, too, despaired, and I took a vow to spend my life as a lowly hermit, fasting and praying for my brother's deliverance. Only the good metalworker Trebuchet continued the quest, leaving me here to my prayers.

"And as I prayed, I asked that I might have some sign by which I might know if my brother would ever be whole, and Ganscotter himself came to me. He said to me that my prayers had been heard, and I should be permitted to see the future, if only I should be willing to give up the past. The past I cared nothing for. I agreed.

"And now, each day, I lose more of my memories and see farther into the future. Soon, I believe I will see what I have so longed to see and forget what I have so longed to forget. This I write, swearing to its truth, and sign with my own name, Sir Trevisant of Munsalvaesche."

Terence put down the book and they all looked at Trevisant, who had fallen into a peaceful sleep. "May he see pleasant things, as he dreams of the world that is to come," Terence said softly.

"So he was a knight," Gawain murmured. Then he looked back at Terence. "What do you make of that tale, Terence?"

Terence shook his head. "Ganscotter we know, of course, but I have heard none of the other names."

"I've heard of the smith, Trebuchet," Gawain commented. "They say that there are no weapons like the ones he made."

"Who is Ganscotter?" Piers asked.

Terence looked at Piers for a long time before answering. "He is my father."

Piers nodded. "I think I understand, now," he said softly.

"You do?" Gawain asked.

Choosing his words with care, Piers described the castle of the Grail – Munsalvaesche, he supposed – and the strange procession that he and Parsifal had witnessed there. He told of the bleeding lance, the flowers and candles, the silver knives of Trebuchet, and finally of the Grail itself. Then he told of Parsifal's silence and the tirade delivered the next morning by the man in motley. "He said that we might have healed the king, but had failed. That was why Parsifal sent me away. I was the one who taught him not to ask questions."

"I see," Terence said.

"And there's one more thing," Piers said. "Your friend Trevisant mentioned his sister, Lady Herzeloyde."

"Yes?" asked Terence.

"That is the name of Parsifal's mother."

8

THE CHÂTEAU MERVEILE

The road through the Gentle Wood went north and south, and since the three travellers had not passed Parsifal on the trail as they came from the south, they decided to continue north. They settled this that evening in Trevisant's cottage, while Trevisant slept fitfully on his bed. When they finished talking, Terence leaned back in his chair and said, "I'm glad you'll have Piers with you, milord."

Gawain smiled. "You'll not be going with us, then?" He did not sound surprised.

Terence glanced at the hermit and shook his head. "I'll catch up with you when I can."

Gawain looked at Piers. "I hope you can cook better than I can, lad."

They left at dawn, Gawain expressing the desire

to catch up with Parsifal as soon as possible. Remembering Parsifal's penchant for riding hard all day, Piers did not think they would, but he said nothing. As they rode through the woods, it struck him that even in his wildest childhood dreams he had never *imagined* going on a quest as the sole companion of the great Sir Gawain, but he only shrugged at the thought. Questing wasn't as glamorous as he had supposed. Nor, in fact, was Gawain, but Piers realized that he much preferred the real Gawain, with his ready smile and casual manners, to the hero of the stories.

Shortly after midday, they rode into a clearing where a lady wearing one of those impractical conical hats with a streamer tied at the top was wailing wretchedly over a knight's body. Seeing Gawain's approach, she wailed louder.

"I pray thee, my lady," said Gawain, after decently allowing her a few moments for grief, "tell me how I may serve thee." The lady did not speak but only cried more brokenly. "Has some other knight slain your...your companion?" Gawain asked doggedly.

"Slain?" the woman said, breaking off in mid-sob, "but he is not slain."

"He's not?"

"But I make no doubt that he soon will be dead!"

she cried, resuming her tears.

Gawain glanced speakingly at Piers, then dismounted. "Perhaps I could take a look at your companion's wounds...ah, I mean, if that's what the trouble is."

"How can you ask such a question?" the woman cried. "Do you not see him bleed?"

"Well, actually, no, I don't see any...oh, do you mean that spot up by the shoulder? Yes, I see." Gawain looked thoughtful. "Is that, ah, his only wound, my lady?"

"Is it not enough?"

"I shouldn't have thought so," Gawain muttered, but the woman didn't hear him, being busy launching another soulful wail. "Let me take his armour off and examine him. I am no doctor, but I have tended wounds before."

Piers dismounted and helped Gawain loosen the fallen knight's armour. When they removed his helm, the man began to moan piteously, but when they had uncovered the wound, they found it to be nothing but a deep scratch in the flesh of the upper arm.

Gawain stood. "I think he'll be fine, my lady."

"But he's lost a vast amount of blood!" she declared.

Gawain glanced quickly around the meadow.

There were no marks of blood on the grass. "Where'd he put it, then?"

The knight promptly fainted away, and the woman began to sob again. "Art thou indeed so heartless, O knight? Have thou pity on us. Send your squire to fetch us healing herbs, or surely my love shall die this very night."

Gawain sighed and glanced at Piers. "Do you know any healing herbs, Piers?"

"No. My mother never used them. Once when I was sick and crying a lot she gave me some of my father's ale."

Gawain grinned. "Did it help?"

"I don't know. I don't remember anything afterwards."

Gawain chuckled and looked back at the lady. "Shall we fetch you some ale, my lady?"

"Ale would not help him recover from his wound!"

"How about some for you, then? I don't know but that I might get a bit for myself."

"Begone, O fiend! How canst thou mock us in our grief? Oh, that someone would bring us some salve to assuage the pain."

Gawain looked skeptically at the knight, but he bowed slightly to the lady. "Truly it was ill done of me to make light of your concern. I'll go look for some herbs. I know a few that are sometimes used."

The lady smiled beatifically. "Or, if you like, you could just ride into the village – it's only half a mile away – and buy some salve at the apothecary's there. He's very knowledgeable."

Gawain frowned. "Only half a mile?"

The lady quickly added, "As you see, O knight, we have no horse but one broken-down nag, and I dared not leave my love, lest he die alone."

Gawain glanced across the clearing, where a sway-backed old mare was tethered. "Ay, very noble of you, I'm sure." He swung into his saddle and looked down at Piers. "You stay here, lad, and give your horse a rest. I'll be back in a few minutes."

When Gawain was gone, Piers led his horse across the clearing, where the grass was thicker, and picketed him near the old mare. For a moment Piers watched the horses graze, then turned back toward the lady. The knight had woken up, and the two were whispering together. Piers decided to leave them alone and found a tree under which to sit.

Gawain returned half an hour later, carrying a small bottle. Piers waved but stayed in the pleasant shade. Gawain waved back, then dismounted.

"Here's your salve, my lady."

"Would you put in on his wound, O knight? I shall faint if I see such gore, I know."

"Yes, of course, my lady." Gawain knelt over the knight's shoulder with his bottle of salve. The lady reached behind a tree, produced a stout branch, and bashed Gawain on the back of the head. Piers could only stare, astonished. The wounded knight leaped to his feet, kicked Gawain's groggy form backward and raced to Guingalet.

"Hurry!" he shouted, when he had mounted. The lady ran up, caught the knight's hand, and swung nimbly up behind him. A moment later, the knight and lady had vanished into the forest on Guingalet, leaving Gawain on his hands and knees, stunned, and Piers still sitting in the shade beneath his tree, nearly as stunned as Gawain.

"Was it the lady?" Gawain asked Piers groggily.

"Yes, sir. She had a big branch hidden behind that tree. When you knelt, she hit you with it. It looked like she hit you hard."

"Thank you, Piers," Gawain said acidly. "I am aware of how hard she hit me. Why didn't you do anything?" Gawain closed his eyes and slowly moved his head back and forth.

"She hit you too quickly for me to stop her,"

Piers said. "Sorry I wasn't any help just then. But I think I can help you now."

"How?" Gawain muttered.

"Well, we have this salve, you see, and I can—"

"Oh, shut up," Gawain moaned. "Where did they go? Which direction?"

Piers pointed. "That way, through the forest."

"Well, they won't get far on that old horse," Gawain said, struggling to his feet. "Let's go ask them what they were about."

Piers didn't move. "Um, they aren't on that old horse, I'm afraid. They rode off on Guingalet."

Piers had expected Gawain to be angry, but instead a faint smile crossed Gawain's face. "That makes it even easier. Come on."

They rode off together, with Piers on his own horse and Gawain riding the sway-backed mare. Piers had offered to ride the nag, but Gawain only waved a hand and said, "It doesn't matter. We'll come up to them soon."

Sure enough, they had gone barely a mile before they came to the lady, afoot beneath a tree. She was crying again.

"Why hello, my dear," Gawain said sweetly.

The woman looked up, recognized Gawain, and immediately stopped crying. "You!"

"Were you expecting someone else? Your

wounded companion, perhaps? Where is he, by the way? Was he just a better rider than you?"

The woman's face twisted, and she glanced quickly above her head. Following her glance up into the thick foliage of the elm tree, Piers saw the knight's gauntleted hands hanging down out of a heavy patch of leaves. Looking more closely, Piers could just make out the rest of the knight, caught in the branches. The hands swayed slightly with the movement of the tree, but otherwise did not move.

Gawain began to laugh. "Why Guingalet, my lad, I'm proud of you! That branch must be eight feet from the ground. Not bad for a middle-aged horse."

"Please, sir," the lady said. "Can you help him? He may be hurt."

"But of course, my lady," Gawain said gallantly. He tossed her the bottle he had purchased. "Here's some salve." He urged the sway-backed horse past the lady, and Piers followed.

For a while they were able to follow Guingalet's tracks in the bare ground of the forest, but then they left the trees and came into a grassy field by a wide river, where they could no longer see the horse's trail. Gawain said, "Let's stay near this river. Guingalet's an aughisky, a water horse. He'd as soon swim as run."

They rode beside the river for almost an hour, and Gawain was getting more and more frustrated. At Piers's suggestion, Gawain removed every easily detached part of his armour, including his helm, breast-plate and shield, and handed them to Piers so as to lighten the load on the mare. Just before the mare gave out entirely, they rounded a bend of the river and saw a majestic castle on the opposite shore and, on this side, a knight sitting on a huge black horse.

"Guingalet!" Gawain called joyfully, urging the mare forward.

"Halt!" called the knight.

Gawain did not stop. "Sorry, sir knight, for the trouble, but that's my horse."

"Nay, sir. It is mine! By right of discovery and conquest, and ne'er have I bestridden so fine a beast."

"Yes, I know. That's why I'm so eager to get him back. He was stolen from me down the way, and we've been chasing him this hour and more. Look, I can prove it. That's my knife in the scabbard on the saddle. It has a carved snake on the haft—"

"I care not!" the knight rapped out. "Though he may have been yours this morning, now he is mine! Or, if you deny it, you may fight me for the horse.

But I must warn you. I am Sir Lejoie, and I have never been unhorsed."

"Oh, very well," Gawain said. "Let me just get my armour and borrow my friend's mount."

He turned toward Piers, and Piers shouted, "Look out, Gawain!"

Sir Lejoie had drawn a lance and had booted Guingalet into a run. Gawain swore and jerked the old mare around to face the oncoming knight. "Get out of the way, Piers!" he hissed, and Piers guided his horse to one side.

Piers looked back just in time to see the battle. Gawain had swiftly positioned the mare at the knight's left and kicked his feet free of the stirrups. He held no lance and made no effort to draw his sword. When Sir Lejoie got to him, Gawain twisted his body sharply so that the lance just missed him. Then he grabbed the lance and, throwing himself from the saddle, rode the lance to the ground. The lance gouged the meadow, stuck, and then shattered. Gawain, who had landed heavily in the turf, rolled swiftly to his feet, drawing his sword. His face was scraped and bloody.

Sir Lejoie, meanwhile, had his own problems. Guingalet had not enjoyed the jolt, and now the great horse had set himself to get rid of his rider.

Sir Lejoie was a good horseman and stayed on Guingalet's back for several seconds, but there was only one possible end to the struggle, and eventually Sir Lejoie left the saddle and landed on his back. He started to sit up, but Gawain's sword was at his throat.

"Now he's *my* horse again," Gawain said.

"You can't do this!" Sir Lejoie said, his voice tight and his face livid. "I've never been defeated! Never!"

"Yes, you have," Gawain said. The sword point did not move.

Sir Lejoie collapsed on his back with a moan. "Kill me," he said.

"What?"

"I said, 'Kill me', for I no longer want to live."

"What, because you took a fall? Don't be an ass."

"Kill me! Kill me!"

"No!" Gawain snapped with irritation. "Oh, get up, you silly sod." Gawain moved his sword away from Sir Lejoie's throat and stepped back.

Immediately, Sir Lejoie leaped to his feet and drew his own sword. "Now we shall see who will win!" he crowed.

Gawain knocked him down and took his sword away. Piers wasn't sure exactly how Gawain had done it, but it was just that fast. One moment Sir

Lejoie was standing in a sword-fighter's crouch, and the next he was on his back again with Gawain's foot on his wrist. When he had plucked the sword from Sir Lejoie's hand, Gawain tossed it Piers. "Here, lad. You can have this now."

Piers caught the sword deftly and looked distastefully at it. "I don't want it. It's trash."

Sir Lejoie started to get up again, but Gawain knocked him down again. "What do you mean, Piers?"

"This sword. It's heavy, unbalanced and made of poor steel. My father makes better swords than this in his sleep. I'll go throw it away." Piers trotted over to the river bank and threw the sword into the water, while Gawain laughed.

"Kill me," moaned Sir Lejoie.

"Oh stop it," Gawain said. "I don't want to kill you; you'll just have to accept that."

A movement to his side drew Piers's attention, and he saw a long, flat raft crossing the river from the castle on the other side. A man with a pole guided it across. "Gawain?" Piers said.

Gawain looked up from Sir Lejoie. "Now who's this, I wonder."

"Why don't you want to kill me?" whined Sir Lejoie. Gawain continued holding him down but otherwise ignored him. In a minute, the boat crunched into the gravel bank, and the boatman stepped off into the meadow. He was tall and austere and had a long gray beard. "I am Mazadan the Ferryman," he said, "and I have come to claim my prize."

Gawain raised one eyebrow. "And what prize is that?"

"It is the custom of this place, carved in stone on the very wall of the Château Merveile behind us, that after every combat that takes place within sight of those towers, I shall be given the horse of the defeated knight."

"Fine," Gawain said, pointing to the old mare. "Take her."

"Nay," Mazadan replied. "That was your horse. This great black horse was ridden by the defeated knight."

Gawain turned his eyes heavenward. "Why does everyone want my horse today?"

"Nay," the ferryman repeated. "This was—"

"Yes, yes, I know, but you see that really was my horse. That's why we were fighting, so that I could get my horse back. So, he really didn't belong to the defeated knight after all."

"Yes, he did," Sir Lejoie interposed.

"You hush!" Gawain snapped. "Ask my friend here. Piers, isn't that my horse?"

Piers said it was, but the ferryman ignored him. "It does not matter," he announced. "That was the horse that was ridden by the loser. That is the custom of the castle."

"How about this?" Gawain said patiently. "You've been getting the horses of losing knights up until now. Wouldn't you rather just once be given the horse of the winner?"

Mazadan looked at the mare and wrinkled his nose. "Not likely," he said.

"Isn't there something else I can give you instead? How about this chucklehead's armour? We've already tossed away his sword, but..." Gawain trailed off and then grinned. "Or how about this? Instead of the loser's horse, why don't I give you the loser?"

"Eh?" Mazadan said.

"He can help you pole the raft. A horse can't do that, you know."

Mazadan hesitated, then nodded. "All right. Fair trade. Come along, boy. I'll have to show you where to stand."

Sir Lejoie stood up. "I say, you can't—"

"Go with him, or I'll knock you down again," Gawain said, and Sir Lejoie turned slowly and followed the ferryman.

Gawain caught Guingalet's reins and began

crooning to the horse in a strange gutteral language, but then was interrupted. Mazadan called out, "Well, hurry up, you two!"

Gawain and Piers exchanged puzzled glances. Then Gawain said, "You mean us?"

"Of course I mean you," Mazadan said. "They're waiting for you at the castle."

When the raft was halfway across the river, Mazadan left his new helper to his task and walked to the front of the raft where Gawain and Piers waited beside the horses. Gawain had put his armour back on, but he had removed his helm, and Piers was cleaning the blood from his scraped face with a wet cloth.

"Ah," Gawain said to Mazadan. "I'd hoped you would come back this way. Who are 'they' who are expecting us in that castle?"

"They who live therein," the ferryman replied.

"That's very helpful. Could you tell us a name, perhaps?"

"No."

"Ah. Well, how about this? What are they expecting us for?"

"To set them free."

Gawain nodded pensively. "If it's not too much to ask, how would I go about doing that?"

"You must face the *lit merveile*."

"The what?" But Mazadan moved away without answering, and Gawain turned to Piers. "Did you catch that?"

"It sounded like French," Piers said hesitantly. "But it doesn't make much sense."

"You speak French?" Gawain asked. Piers nodded. "Good. Did it sound as if he said *'lit merveile'* to you?"

Piers nodded. "Yes. 'The wonderful bed'."

"That's what I thought." Gawain shrugged. "We'll find out soon, I suppose." They arrived at the bank of the river beside the great open gate of the castle. Gawain said, "No point in waiting. Let's go look for something odd and French." He leaped lightly onto the beach, and Piers followed.

They entered the gate, but the courtyard was empty. Gawain stopped and looked around. "I see no one, but the castle is well kept. Even the flagstones are swept." Piers looked at a stone carving of a lion on the wall, and for an instant the carving blurred, as if Piers's eyes had suddenly begun to water, but then his vision cleared again. Piers rubbed his eyes and saw Gawain do the same. "Are your eyes blurry, Gawain?" Piers asked.

"Just for a moment," Gawain replied. "They're fine now. Come on."

Next it was a moulded cornice that grew momentarily indistinct, then a stairway. "Gawain?"

Gawain had stopped moving and was looking around him. "Ay, lad?"

"Something's happening. I'm scared."

"I see them, too. Either my eyes are going bad or the castle is behaving oddly. Or else ... or else something keeps passing before my eyes."

They continued through the castle. Every door was open, every passageway clean and empty, but for the vague flitting motions that never went away, as if someone were pulling an almost-invisible silken screen through the air, blurring everything it passed in front of. It was a beautiful castle, filled with lovely furniture, but Piers found himself praying that they could leave before it got dark. The Château Merveile was scary enough in the daylight.

They were now deep in the central *donjon*, the tower that stood at the castle's heart, and there was less light. Piers pressed closer to Gawain, who touched Piers's shoulder reassuringly. Then they stepped into the strangest room Piers had ever seen. It was at least forty feet from floor to ceiling, perfectly round, and completely without windows. The only light was from a ring of torches high on the wall above them. In the very centre of the room was a rough and rustic bed.

"A bed," Gawain said. "Do you think that's it? 'The wonderful bed'?"

"It . . . it looks pretty ordinary," Piers ventured.

"Ay, the most normal thing we've seen yet in this ghastly place," Gawain assented. He drew his sword and walked slowly around the bed, examining it from every angle. "I feel a bit silly, arming myself against furniture," he commented.

"Maybe there's something else in this room," Piers suggested. Together they walked around and examined the walls. There were regular holes in the stones of the wall, but they were far too small for any enemies to get through.

"Deuced if I understand it," Gawain said. "But there's one thing. Since we came in this room I haven't seen any of those boggarts flitting about. Maybe we're actually safer in here than out there."

Still looking around him, Gawain sat on the edge of the bed, and then there was no more talk of being safe. The moment that he touched the bed, the door through which they had entered slammed closed and the bed began to move. Gawain grabbed quickly at the bedpost, dropping his sword on the floor, and then the bed was off – careening into walls and bouncing off, with

Gawain grimly holding on to the headboard. Three times Piers had to throw himself to one side to escape being crushed between the bed and the stone wall, and Piers realized he needed to be on the bed, too. The next time the bed came toward him, Piers threw himself beside Gawain, who grabbed him and pulled him up.

"C'est un lit merveile!" Gawain called.

"You don't say," Piers snapped back. His foot was throbbing where the bedpost had bashed it when he jumped on, and Gawain's shield, still looped onto Gawain's forearm, kept rapping him in the face. He did not feel like making clever French conversation.

They rode the bed about the room for another minute before Gawain called out, "There's something moving on the wall!" Piers looked and saw what Gawain meant, but the bed was moving too fast to make out what it was. "Blast!" Gawain shouted. "Get under my shield, Piers! Now!"

Piers curled his body into as tight a ball as he could, considering the jolting he was taking, and tried to get as much of his body under the shield as possible. At once the shield began to ping and thunk with hundreds of sharp blows. Something hit Piers hard in the small of the back, and he pressed himself closer to Gawain and under the shield. "What are they?" Piers shouted.

"Stones! From slings!" Gawain called back.

After a moment the hail of stones stopped, and Piers ventured to peek out from under the shield. A short, thick shaft of wood zipped over him, nipping his scarlet hat from his head and pinning it neatly to the headboard. "Crossbows!" Gawain shouted. "Back under the shield!" Then the hail of missiles began again, but even more deadly this time, for every crossbow shaft that hit Gawain's shield stuck and went through it to a length of at least four inches. Soon the shield was like a giant's pincushion. More than once Piers heard Gawain grunt with pain, and he tried to push the shield over to cover the knight better, but Gawain pushed it back. "I . . . have . . . armour," he gasped.

It seemed hours, but in fact was probably no more than a minute, before the crossbows stopped, and when they ceased, the bed stopped as well. "Gawain?" Piers asked after a moment.

"I must be alive," Gawain said hoarsely. "Dead doesn't hurt this much."

Piers crawled out from under the shield and looked around. There was blood on both of Gawain's arms, and several crossbow shafts that had managed to pierce his armour stuck out like hedgehog quills. Stiffly, Gawain got off the bed and looked around on the floor until he found his sword. Piers tugged three bolts out of the headboard and rescued his hat. All the plumes had been torn away, and with its new holes the hat was beginning to look decidedly ragged.

"I don't know what's next, lad, but stay near me," Gawain said. He unslung his arrow-studded shield and threw it onto the bed, just as an enormous cat with a heavy ring of hair around its face came through the door. Piers had never seen a live lion before, but he knew one when he saw it.

The lion roared and launched itself at Gawain. Gawain's sword flashed, and Piers saw blood spurt from one of the cat's paws, but the other paw knocked Gawain stumbling backwards. The lion roared again, louder, and limped toward Gawain. Gawain heaved himself to his feet and moved away. For a minute the knight and the lion both limped in a circle. Then the lion leaped again. Gawain lifted his sword, but his feet slipped beneath him in a pool of the lion's blood, and the lion landed right on top of him. Gawain's sword skittered across the room, and Piers screamed, "No!"

Grabbing the only weapon he could find, Gawain's ruined shield, Piers ran toward the lion and threw himself against it. For a few wild moments the lion roared and thrashed while Piers pushed the shield against the lion's side, and then Piers was thrown through the air against a wall. His head rang, and he slid down the wall onto a litter of bloody stones and broken crossbow bolts.

"Is he dead?" a voice asked. It was a woman's voice. Piers opened his eyes and saw two ladies standing over the lion's body. Gawain was nowhere to be seen. One of the ladies knelt and bowed her head. Piers saw her lips move and realized she was praying. Shaking with weariness, Piers stood.

"What have you done with Gawain?" he said softly.

"He is under the lion," the standing lady said. Staggering over, Piers saw that the lady was right. The lion's body almost completely covered Gawain's form.

"Gawain?" he whispered.

"Mmpf," said Gawain.

9

THE GARLAND
FROM THE RIVER

By the time Piers and the two ladies had pulled the
dead lion completely off him, Gawain had fainted.
Wordlessly, they worked together to remove
Gawain's battered armour and determine the
extent of his wounds. They were many but not
severe. The crossbow bolts had not been able to
penetrate the double layer of armour around
Gawain's torso, so all of his wounds were on his
arms and legs. One lady brought a basin of water,
and together the ladies bathed his wounds.

The ladies seemed to know what to do, so Piers
left them to their work and looked around. There
were at least a dozen women peeking around
the doorway, watching the proceedings. A few
blushed when Piers looked at them, but most

smiled with a friendliness that was touched with gratitude. Piers wondered where all these women had been hiding when he and Gawain had searched the castle.

At last Gawain's wounds were washed and bound, and one of the two ladies – a graceful woman with long, straight black hair that flowed over her shoulders like a waterfall – called for a pallet. Several of the ladies hurried away, and soon they were gently lifting Gawain onto a thin, hard cot. "We'll give him a more restful bed this time, I think," the lady with black hair said. Eight of the ladies lifted Gawain, bed and all, and took him out. Then the dark-haired lady turned to Piers. "And you will be weary as well. Please come with me, and I'll take you to a room near Gawain's."

"Thank you," Piers replied humbly. "I am very tired. But please, can you tell me what all this is? Who are you? Where did you come from?"

"In good time, Piers."

"You know my name? But how?"

"In good time." They started to leave, but Piers could barely walk on the ankle that had been hit by the bedpost. Seeing his limp, the lady took Piers's arm and supported him down the hall to an elegantly furnished bedchamber. There she guided him to a chair by a cheery fire, then knelt at his feet and examined his ankle. "I think it is not broken," she said at last, "but it is very swollen. You should rest now and try not to walk on it."

"Yes, my lady," Piers said. He could not imagine arguing with this majestic person. "Thank you, my lady."

"You may call me Nimue," she said.

"Nimue!" Piers exclaimed. "Then you are... ah... do you have... do you have a daughter named Ariel?"

"I do have an impetuous, willful and incurably inquisitive daughter by that name," the woman said gravely.

"She... she told me that you were the most beautiful creature in any world," Piers said.

Nimue laughed, and her laughter was like a mountain brook dancing over stones. "I'll send her in to you after you've rested," Nimue promised. Then she left, and Piers decided it would be easier to sleep in his chair by the fire than to bother moving again, so he did.

"Piers?" the whispered voice was disturbing his dreams, and Piers tried to ignore it, but it only came back, louder this time. "Pi-ers? Oh, Pi-ers." Piers opened his eyes, and there was Ariel. She smiled happily at him. "Mother said I must let you sleep, but you were about to wake up anyway, weren't you?"

"It doesn't matter," Piers murmured. "I'd rather be awake now anyway."

Ariel smiled more brightly and turned pink. "Mother told me all that you've done. I think it's wonderful! Did you really attack that lion all by yourself? I didn't know you were so brave! I mean I knew you were probably brave, but I didn't know how much."

"I wasn't really attacking him," Piers said. "I just wanted him to get off Gawain."

"But he could have killed you," Ariel said, her eyes wide.

"I didn't really think about that," Piers admitted. "Say, do you know what that was all about?"

"You mean the bed and the lion and all?" Piers nodded, and Ariel returned his nod gleefully. "Yes. Mother told me just an hour ago, and she said that I might tell you too, as soon as you woke up, which is why I just looked in to see if you were awake, and you weren't, but you looked as though you might wake up soon, so I came on in. You *were* about to wake up, weren't you?"

Piers laughed. "I guess so. I'm awake, aren't I?"

"Well, that's what I thought. Shall I tell you now, or would you rather go back to sleep?"

"Oh, hurry up, will you?" Piers said.

"Well, this castle is called the 'Château Merveile'. It's one of the castles of ladies. There are several of them in this world. Of course, it's not the greatest of them, but—"

"Hold on," Piers said. "What do you mean 'this world'? Are we in—?"

"Don't you even know?" Ariel asked, giggling. "You're in the Other World now, of course. You came over on the ferry. Isn't that funny? A ferry to the faeries. Now don't interrupt any more, or I'll forget the order of the story."

"Sorry." Piers looked around him. It didn't *look* like another world, but then he'd never seen another world before, so he could be wrong.

"Anyway, as I was saying, this is one of the castles of ladies—"

"You mean only ladies live here?"

"That's right."

"Why?"

"Well, they have to live somewhere, don't they? Are you going to keep interrupting?"

"Sorry," Piers said, but then he added quickly, "One more thing before you get started. Where were all these ladies when Gawain and I got here? We looked everywhere."

"I'll tell you if you'll just be quiet," Ariel said

patiently. "Anyway, this castle has two hundred ladies in it, and there was this enchanter named Gottfried who wanted to come here."

Piers frowned. "Why?"

"What do you mean, why?"

"I mean, why would a man want to go live somewhere where there were only women? It sounds terrible. Two hundred women always telling him to pick up his stockings and clean his nails."

Ariel frowned thoughtfully. "Well, I don't know exactly, but Mother says that men are always trying to get in. Maybe they're in love."

"With two hundred at once?" Piers asked sceptically. "This Gottfried can't have thought it through."

"Maybe not," Ariel said. "But that's what he wanted, anyway. And he tried and tried to get in using his magic, but every time he tried he failed."

"We didn't have any trouble getting in," Piers observed. "Didn't this Gottfried notice that the gate was open?"

"I don't know," Ariel said, with a touch of irritation. "I don't know why Gottfried couldn't force his way in while you just walked in, but that's what my mother told me. Do you want to hear this story or not?"

"I'm sorry," Piers said contritely. "I'll listen now."

"Thank you. So after Gottfried had tried everything and failed, he was very angry and he cast a curse over the whole castle. He said that since he couldn't enter and see the ladies of the castle, no one should see them." Piers frowned, puzzled, but was careful not to speak. Ariel explained, "He made the women invisible, like ghosts. So you see, they were all around you when you got here, but you just couldn't see them."

Piers shivered and glanced involuntarily about the room. Ariel giggled. "They're all better, now, silly. And there's another part of the curse. Gottfried said that if he was to be denied a bed in this castle, then it would be a bed that held them captive. So he cast a magic spell and made the marvellous bed appear in the middle hall, and then he arranged for all the other things, like the slings and the crossbows and the lion."

"But that doesn't make sense!" Piers protested, unable to stay silent any longer. "How could he do all that when he wasn't even able to magic his way into the castle? I mean, how could he get this wretched bed and this lion in but not himself?"

Ariel smiled ruefully. "That's just what I asked

Mother when she told me the story. She said that magicians who are good at making curses aren't much good at anything else. Maybe he had only one kind of magic."

"The nastiest kind," Piers said. "And Gawain and I just walked right in without any trouble, and Gawain broke the spell."

"You can't say *that* was without any trouble," Ariel pointed out. "Mother says that Sir Gawain had more than twenty wounds."

Piers leaped to his feet, wincing as he put his weight on his ankle. In his pleasure at seeing Ariel, he had not even thought of Gawain. "Where is he? Can you take me to him?"

Ariel hesitated, then nodded. "Well, all right. He's just next door. You . . . you won't tell anyone that I woke you up, will you? I mean, if there's someone with him."

Piers promised, and then limped behind Ariel into a corridor and on to the next door. Ariel opened it gently and peeked in. Looking over Ariel's head, Piers saw Nimue sitting beside a bed where Gawain lay asleep. "Excuse me, Mother," Ariel whispered. "Piers woke up and wanted to see Sir Gawain."

Nimue's eyes narrowed, and she looked suspiciously at her daughter. Piers stretched elaborately and said, "I had a very good rest, ma'am."

Nimue's lips quivered. "Very well," she said at last. Your friend is asleep, but you may come and see him."

The next few weeks were a time of sheer pleasure for Piers. While Gawain recovered from his wounds and slowly regained his strength, and as soon as Piers's ankle was better, he and Ariel climbed the castle's battlements, explored the cellars (to their shared disappointment they found no secret doors or hidden passageways, no matter how hard they looked), and swam in the river. Ariel was like a fish in the water, but more graceful. Piers felt peaceful and secure as he had not since he left home.

Sitting on the riverbank with Ariel, tossing pebbles into the current, Piers talked about his home. He told about his grand, proud, laughing mother and his sombre, but (Piers had since realized) equally proud father. He described to her the fine metalwork that his father had in his shop, and he realized that he missed the forge. "I wish I had paid more attention to my father, but all I could think of was being a squire, or at least a page."

Ariel hugged her knees, still damp from a swim, and looked curiously at Piers. "Being a page is an honourable life," she commented.

"Yes," Piers said. "But when you're done at the end of the day, you haven't anything to show for it."

Ariel looked sceptical, but all she said was, "Are you ready for another swim?"

Piers agreed at once. "Let's race to that island over there. I get a head start."

Ariel shook her head. "No, we aren't permitted on that island." Piers gave her a questioning look, but Ariel answered, "I don't know. Mother just said not to swim over there."

A few nights later, Piers was walking on the battlements with Ariel and Nimue, and as they walked in view of the island, Piers stopped and looked at it. "Nimue?" he asked.

"Yes?"

"What is on that island? Why are we not to swim there?"

Nimue leaned on the wall and looked at Piers fondly. "You have grown up quite a bit since you started your quest, Piers. The old Piers would have been afraid to ask questions." Piers thought of Parsifal and of their failure at Munsalvaesche, and he felt a twist of guilt. Nimue continued, "That is

192

where the Questing Garland is kept."

"The what?"

"There is a garden in the centre of that island, and on the tree in the middle of that garden hangs a garland of sweet flowers. Whoever has that garland is sure to find whatever he seeks."

Piers stared at Nimue, then stared back at the island. In the growing night, it was little more than a patch of blackness in the gray river, but he stared at it as if he could catch a glimpse of the magic garland.

"But it is not so easy as all that," Nimue added. "First, there is a knight who guards it, both day and night. And second, and most important, the garland is useless to the one who takes it. It will not work unless it is given away."

Piers puzzled over this for a minute. "You mean if . . . Gawain or someone went and took the garland, it wouldn't help him on his quest, but if someone else took it and gave it to . . . to Gawain or someone, then it would help him find what he looks for."

Nimue's smile shone briefly in the gloom. "That's right. It is always the way in this world. Whatever you seize for yourself is worthless; only what is given to you has value. That is why you and Gawain could walk into this castle without trouble, while that poor, silly magician Gottfried could not force his way in by any means under the sun. Come, let us walk on."

The three continued on their stroll, but Piers looked over his shoulder at the dark island, and his heart beat furiously in his breast.

It was after midnight when Piers stole into Gawain's room. He did not want to disturb the knight, but he felt that he ought to have a sword, and Gawain's was the only one that he knew of. The sword slid easily into Piers's hand, and for a moment Piers marvelled at how light and well-balanced it was. His interest roused, he promised himself that he would examine the sword more closely in the daylight, if he ever saw daylight again.

A minute later he had run silently down to the castle stables, where Guingalet snorted a surly welcome. The great horse was restless and in need of exercise, and it took Piers almost half an hour to saddle him and lead him out into the courtyard. Piers glanced nervously at the windows that lined the court, but there was no light except from the half-moon overhead. In a moment he and the horse were out of the castle at the river bank.

"All right, old fellow," Piers hissed to the horse.

"Your master says that you're at home in the water. Let's see." Taking a deep breath, Piers climbed into the saddle. He felt Guingalet's muscles bunch, but the horse did not try to throw him. Piers let his breath out with a sigh. At Piers's direction, the horse plunged into the river. The water was unnaturally cold, or at least seemed that way in the darkness, and Piers clenched his teeth with the shock of it. When the water surged past his armpits, he lost his grip on the reins and had to grab the horse's mane to keep from falling, but he kept his grip on Gawain's sword. He hoped that Guingalet was going the right direction.

After a very long time, Guingalet lurched up, his hooves having struck the gravelly shore. Piers could not tell if this was the island or the opposite riverbank, but it seemed to be about the right distance from the dark mass of the castle behind him. He tethered Guingalet to a dead tree that lay on the bank and walked resolutely into the blackness of the woods.

Reminding himself that he was not a child anymore and was far too old to be frightened of the dark helped for a little while, but when things skittered through the brush at his feet, he still jumped, and his heart still pounded wildly.

Thorny branches clawed at his clothes, and twice he had to stop and disentangle his hat from their briars. This was no garden, Piers reflected, but he pushed on. The wind moaned in a hollow tree beside him, and Piers's legs felt weak. He took several deep breaths and reminded himself severely that if he was going to be afraid, he should be afraid of the very real knight who guarded the garland and not of imaginary horrors.

He stumbled out of the underbrush and found himself in a level grassy clearing. The black trees, stark against the grey night sky, formed a perfect circle around the open area. This must be the garden. Piers looked anxiously about, but he saw nothing moving. He raised Gawain's sword and slowly began to walk toward the centre of the garden. Rounding a dark hedge, he stubbed his toe on something hard, and fell on his face.

"Who's there?" demanded a rough voice. Piers leaped to his feet, and saw a human shape rise from the ground. Piers had tripped over a resting knight. "Who are you?" the knight said.

"I'm . . . nobody, sir," Piers stammered.

"Why are you here?" the knight demanded. The knight was as large as Gawain. "Why do you disturb my sleep?"

Piers hesitated, then replied honestly. "I was

looking for an enchanted garland that will help someone achieve his quest."

"This is the place," the knight said, and he drew his sword. "I am its guardian."

Piers swallowed and held his own sword ready. "I understand, sir," he said.

The knight lowered his sword. "How old are you, boy?"

"Twelve, sir."

"Go away. I do not fight children."

"But I need the garland," Piers said.

"Nevertheless, I am sworn to defend it," the knight said. "And you cannot have it. It's hanging right over my head, and I will not move."

Piers looked up, and there it was, hanging from a thin branch of a slender sapling. The moon came out from behind a cloud suddenly, and in the white light Piers saw a vague pinkish tinge on the flowers. He saw something else, too. There was a long, exposed leather strap that extended from the knight's helm to his breastplate. It was like the armour that Sir Ither had been wearing when he rode up to Piers's father's forge. Piers thought quickly back to that scene. His father had scoffed at the armour and had pointed out that the leather strap was a fatal flaw in its design. Piers lowered his sword.

"All right, sir," he said. "Since you're in armour, and I am not, I suppose I have no choice."

"That's a sensible boy," the knight said. He, too, lowered his sword, and Piers leaped forward, stretching Gawain's sword out as far as he could reach. Had Gawain's sword been heavier or clumsier, Piers's inexperienced hands could never have aimed right, but the sword went true. With a quick slash, Piers cut through the leather strap that held the helm in place.

The knight stepped quickly backwards and raised his sword again, but almost at once his hands went to his helm. Without its tether, the helm was loose on the knight's head, and it was already twisted to one side, making it hard for the knight to see. Piers ran forward, leaped up and grasped the garland, then sprinted back into the forest. He heard the knight shout behind him, but then he was in the woods where his size and quickness were to his advantage. All Piers had to do now was find Guingalet.

It took longer than he'd expected. The branches and briars whipped at his face and, again, tore at his hat, but at last Piers stumbled out of the woods onto the shore, where Guingalet stood waiting. Piers jerked the reins free from the log and threw himself into the saddle. As if he sensed Piers's urgency, Guingalet bunched his mighty muscles and launched himself into the river. Horse and rider landed with a terrific splash, and both sank for a moment completely under the surface. Panicking, Piers flailed about and lost his grip on the garland. Then Guingalet began to swim, and Piers's head came out of the water. To his left, already moving away on the current, was the garland, and Piers lunged for it, grabbing it just before it disappeared. Another few seconds of frantic splashing and Piers was back in Guingalet's saddle, garland in one hand, sword in the other.

And far away to the left, bright in the moonlight but disappearing quickly downstream, bobbed Piers's scarlet hat.

Shivering in his wet clothes, Piers rubbed Guingalet dry in the castle stable, then hurried back to his room. There he carefully hid the garland before creeping into Gawain's room to return the sword. The sun was just rising above the horizon as he slid the great sword back into its scabbard, and in the light of the new day Piers saw a curious design at the very end of the sword's hilt. It was a familiar mark, an elaborate letter T.

Two days later, now being well enough for some exercise, Gawain joined Piers for a stroll on the battlements overlooking the river. Piers had been waiting his chance to ask Gawain where he had gotten his sword. Gawain smiled softly. "It was a gift, of course."

"Who from? Did the blacksmith who made it...?"

"No simple blacksmith ever made this sword, Piers," Gawain said with a laugh. "This is the Sword Galatine, and it was given to me years ago by none other than Nimue herself. There is no sword like it, save only Arthur's Excalibur."

"Did Nimue say where she got—"

"Hang on, Piers," Gawain said abruptly. "What's going on across the river?"

Piers looked. In the broad field where Gawain had defeated Sir Lejoie and had recovered Guingalet, a long line of knights had just pulled up. There were pennants, and in the distance Piers could see wagons and still more knights.

"It's too far to make out the heraldry," Gawain mused. "But this is no simple hunting party. That looks like an army. Come on, Piers."

Over Piers's protests, Gawain put on his chain mail, belted on his sword, and headed toward the stables. "Look, Gawain, you can't go facing an army by yourself. What good can you do?" Piers argued as they crossed the courtyard.

"I'm just going to ask these people what they want, Piers, and let them know that there is at least one knight here ready to defend the castle."

"That should scare them," Piers muttered. "I suppose I'd better go with you. Get your gear, and I'll meet you back here."

Piers hurried back to his own room, collected his few possessions and carefully packed the Questing Garland, then joined Gawain at the gate. Together they rode out to where Mazadan and the sullen Sir Lejoie stood by their ferry. Mazadan met them and agreed to take them across. There was a low mist rising from the river, which was actually quite a thick fog at the very centre, but before long they were across. They led their horses off the ferry onto the shore, and Piers glanced behind him. "Gawain!" he gasped.

"What is it?" Gawain said quickly. His sword was in his hand.

"The castle! It's gone!" Behind them was only a river. There was no ferry, no ferryman, and no Château Merveile.

Gawain put his sword back in its sheath. "It looks as if we've made the crossing back to the World of Men," he said quietly. "Shall we go see what we've drawn?"

10

THE KNIGHT IN THE SNOW

Piers and Gawain walked together up the foggy riverbank toward the field where they had seen the knights setting up camp. There was no wind, but a bitter cold settled over Piers, and he began to shiver. "Gawain, I'm cold."

"Ay," Gawain said. "It seems to be winter in this world."

"But how can that be? It was late spring when we left it just a fortnight ago."

Gawain chuckled. "Once Terence and I spent a few months in the Other World, and when we crossed back, found that seven years had passed. You never know how things are moving along when you're away." Gawain stopped suddenly. "Hush!"

Piers halted and listened. Through the fog came

the sound of a man's voice, raised in an angry tirade. "Gawain?" said Piers, "I think I've heard that voice before."

"You have, Piers. That sounds like Kai. Let's go see."

And so it was. Gawain led Piers up to the camp, and a voice called out, "Who's that?"

"Is that you, Dinadan?" Gawain asked. "It's Gawain and Piers the pageboy."

"So you've turned up again, have you?" the voice replied. "I thought maybe this time I'd get my chance to write that funeral dirge I've been planning for you. I've a lovely melody in mind."

"Maybe next time. Is Arthur in the camp?"

"Ay. We're off to Oxford this time. Hardly worthwhile to have a castle at all, the way we're always wandering off to the provinces." The knight's voice had a mocking tone, but then he added, more seriously, "The king will be glad to see you."

"What's all this jabbering?" snapped Sir Kai, who had approached unseen through the fog. "If you fought half as well as you talk, Dinadan —"

"Perish the thought!" Sir Dinadan replied lightly. "Talking's safer. I was just greeting the returned prodigal." Sir Dinadan bowed deeply to Gawain and waved an arm at Sir Kai. "O prodigal, behold the fatted calf."

Sir Kai growled and stepped toward Sir Dinadan, but Gawain said, "Hello, Kai," and Sir Kai halted.

"Gawain?"

"Ay. Could you take me to Arthur?"

King Arthur received them with pleasure, but Sir Kai showed no sign of sharing the king's feelings, especially when Gawain admitted that, while he had had many adventures, he had not found the red knight.

"You haven't?" Sir Kai said with a snort. "Well, what use are all the adventures in the world if you don't do what you set out to do?"

Gawain glanced at Sir Kai and raised his eyebrows, but the king spoke calmly. "I shall be very glad to hear of your travels, nephew. You are welcome." Then the king turned to Piers. "As are you, friend. Forgive me, but have you, ah, mislaid your hat?"

Gawain turned toward Piers. "Say, that's right. What have you done with your red hat?"

"I lost it," Piers said quietly.

King Arthur turned to Gawain. "And where is Terence?"

"We left him along the way," Gawain replied.

Sir Kai snorted. "Can't even keep up with everyone you took with you, much less find that cursed knight."

Gawain and Piers travelled with the royal procession toward Oxford, where Arthur intended to celebrate the Christmas feast. It was a three-day journey, and by the second day, Piers had learned from the other servants in the company that it was best to stay out of Sir Kai's orbit. The seneschal was in a constant state of ill temper.

Piers witnessed Sir Kai's temper himself on the evening of the second day. He was bringing a load of firewood back from the forest when he heard Sir Kai's voice. Mindful of the other servants' warnings, Piers stepped into the shadow of a large holly bush. "You should not be out here alone, my lady," Sir Kai said abruptly to someone Piers could not see.

"You are right," replied a woman's voice. "I should not be out here alone."

There was a long pause, then Sir Kai said, "I only meant it was not safe. There may be wolves in the forest."

"How thoughtful of you," the lady said, her tone ironic. "I suppose you'd rather I was back in the tent with the other ladies, discussing fashions and furbelows."

"You *would* be safer there."

"I'd rather be eaten by wolves. Leave me alone."

Sir Kai's voice, which had grown comparatively gentle, became harsh again. "Let me tell you, Lady Connoire, that there's nothing I'd rather do than leave you alone. But if you get eaten, I'll get the blame for it, just as I get the blame for everything else that happens to you."

The woman laughed. "You mean like when you got blamed for the time that you slapped me in the face? Oh, such injustice!" she retorted.

"Sometimes I think my only mistake was that I didn't hit you hard enough," snapped Sir Kai. He turned on his heel and stalked back to the camp. Lady Connoire watched him go. As soon as Sir Kai was out of sight, she raised her chin and followed him. Piers let his breath out in a long sigh, then followed them both.

They reached Oxford early on the third day. Although it was snowing, the king set up a tent camp outside the city walls by the main road. Piers soon saw why. Crowds of townsmen and peasants began to gather to pay homage to the king or to ask him for a boon. King Arthur was holding court for the common people among his subjects. It was a busy time for King Arthur and his closest advisors, including Sir Kai, but the other members of the royal company were free to wander about as they wished. For a while Piers listened to Sir Dinadan sing a long ballad about Sir Tristram, but although Sir Dinadan sang well and played his stringed rebec with considerable skill, Piers soon lost interest and wandered away to watch the king's farrier at work.

Just at dusk, as Sir Kai was dismissing the crowd outside King Arthur's tent, and knights and ladies were beginning to make their way into the city to the banquet hall of Oxford Castle for the Christmas feast, Piers came upon a sudden commotion. A small group was clustered together, pointing across a snow-covered field, and whispering together: "Do you think it's a challenge?" "Then why doesn't he move?" "Shouldn't we tell the king?"

At the far edge of the field, by a snowdrift, a solitary knight sat on his horse. Though he was far away and in the shadow of a huge spruce, something in his bearing spoke of many miles and great weariness. The knight held a lance, unadorned, but he did not move. He almost seemed to be asleep.

"Well, dash it all," muttered a knight beside Piers. It was an affable and rather portly knight whose name, Piers had learned, was Sir Sagramore. Sir Sagramore alone of all the group was in armour. "We can't just ignore him, and you lads in your party clothes can't go and face him. One of you tell Arthur what's about, and I'll go see what this quiet chap wants. Give me a lance, someone."

A minute later, Sir Sagramore was riding across the white field. As he drew near, the strange knight moved for the first time, lowering his lance carelessly to point at Sir Sagramore's chest. Sir Sagramore halted, and Piers could hear him calling something to the knight, but the knight neither answered nor moved his lance. At last Sir Sagramore's patience ended, and he lowered his own lance and charged. At first the strange knight did not move at all, but then he shifted his weight slightly and urged his tired horse into a slow trot, and then Sir Sagramore flew from his horse's back and landed heavily in the snow.

The crowd at Arthur's camp was accustomed to seeing the finest jousting in the kingdom, but at this casual unseating of Sir Sagramore, a hush fell over them all. Piers heard a low whistle behind him and then Gawain's voice saying, "That, my boy, was not so easy as yon knight made it look. I wonder who the fellow is."

Piers answered immediately. When the strange knight had trotted forward, Piers had seen his armour clearly. "It's Parsifal," he said.

"Parsifal? The red knight?" Gawain exclaimed. People nearby heard, and an excited buzz rose from the growing crowd. By this time everyone knew about the mysterious knight who sent his vanquished foes to Lady Connoire. Piers watched Parsifal return to his spot in the shadows and again become immobile. Sir Sagramore rose from the snowdrift into which he had fallen and, casting one look at the silent knight, limped back to the camp. The murmuring stopped as Sir Sagramore approached, and everyone leaned forward to hear what Sir Sagramore would say.

The portly knight removed his helm and looked ruefully at his eager audience. "That should teach him a lesson," he said.

A sudden clatter of hoof-beats came from the camp, and the onlookers made way for a knight on horseback carrying a lance. It was Sir Kai. "Is it true?" Sir Kai demanded. "Is it the red knight?" When this was confirmed, Sir Kai lowered his helm, pointed his lance, and started across the field.

"Go ahead, Kai," Sir Sagramore called. "I've taken the edge off him for you."

Piers caught his breath, fearing for Parsifal. He had dispatched Sir Sagramore very neatly and, to all appearances, without effort, but Sir Kai was a different matter. Once again, Parsifal seemed to be oblivious of the attacking knight until the last minute, when he lowered his lance, spurred his mount forward, and struck Sir Kai so solidly that Piers heard Sir Kai's grunt, even across the distance. As if he had ridden into a low tree branch, Sir Kai flew over his horse's hindquarters and landed awkwardly on his side. Parsifal returned to the shadows, and Sir Kai lay still.

"Well, go and help him, somebody!" demanded a woman's voice. It was Lady Connoire. Two knights hurried across the snow to where Sir Kai lay, and then one ran back.

"His arm's broken for sure, maybe his leg, too," the knight said. Lady Connoire, standing beside Piers, uttered a very unladylike oath and began to stride across the field. The knight who had returned gathered several men and took a hard pallet from a nearby tent, and they followed her.

Now King Arthur himself arrived. He stilled the hubbub of excited explanations, then turned to Gawain and asked what had transpired.

Gawain told him. "So this is Parsifal," the king said softly. "And why do you suppose he is attacking us?"

"He isn't," Gawain said immediately. "All he's done is defend himself. Piers, go get my horse."

"You're not in armour," the king said. "You can't fight like that."

"I don't intend to fight," Gawain said.

Piers fetched Guingalet, but he brought his own horse as well. Gawain glanced at it and raised his eyebrows. "We started on this quest together," Piers said. Gawain nodded, and they mounted.

They rode slowly across the field, past the churned up places where two different knights had disturbed the snow, right up to where Parsifal sat. He was still in the same position. Now that they were closer, Piers could see that Parsifal was staring fixedly at a spot in the field where three holly berries lay bright against the snow.

"Sir knight?" Gawain said. Parsifal didn't answer. "Sir knight?" Gawain repeated. Then again. Still there was no reply. Gawain cleared his throat loudly and said, "Excuse me," but Parsifal did not move. Gawain glanced at Piers. "He's not hard of hearing, is he?" he asked mildly.

Piers looked at his former master. The armour was battered almost beyond recognition.

Parsifal's mighty shoulders were stooped, and his head hung with evident weariness. And suddenly Piers knew where Parsifal's thoughts had taken him. "The snow is as white as Queen Conduiramour's cheek," Piers said.

"And the berries are as red as her lips when she smiles," Parsifal replied softly. Slowly, Parsifal turned his head and looked at them through his visor. Then he removed his helm and looked again at Piers.

"Pierre?"

Piers shook his head. "No, that was all silly make-believe. My real name is Piers."

Parsifal's face was gaunt and marked with deep lines of exhaustion. "You've lost your hat," he said.

"I was finished with it anyway," Piers replied.

"You look older now."

"So do you. Parsifal, this is Sir Gawain, of King Arthur's court."

Parsifal looked for the first time at Gawain. "You're the knight I wrestled that time."

"That's right," Gawain said. "I've come to take you to King Arthur to be made a knight."

Parsifal took a breath, then shrugged. "All right," he said indifferently. Piers and Gawain turned their horses and led Parsifal out from under the trees. Parsifal reined in his horse suddenly. "Wait," he said. "Look at this." He pointed to the places where Sir Sagramore and Sir Kai had fallen. "Someone's been fighting here recently," he said.

Gawain eyes widened, and a reluctant smile spread across his face. "You mean you don't recall?"

"Recall what? Are you saying I did this?"

"Good Gog," Gawain said. "You beat them both in your sleep."

Back at King Arthur's camp, they encountered a scene very like one that Piers well remembered. Sir Kai lay stretched out on the ground, shaking his head groggily, while the Lady Connoire gently bathed his temples with a damp cloth and King Arthur stood nearby. When they approached and Lady Connoire saw Parsifal with them, she stood and glared at him.

"Just what do you think you were doing, sap-skull?" she demanded. Parsifal looked at her with mild interest, but he did not reply. "Why did you do this?" she continued, waving one arm at Sir Kai's prone form.

"I can only suppose it was because he attacked me," Parsifal replied. "Is he badly hurt?"

"His arm is broken, and his leg badly twisted, thanks to you!"

Parsifal looked at Sir Kai sympathetically. "Is there something I can do to make him more comfortable?" he asked.

Lady Connoire's eyes grew fierce. "You do something for him? Of all the...no, you most certainly cannot. You've done quite enough! Not only have you harmed his body, but you have insulted him repeatedly!"

"Have I?"

"Forty-one times, to be exact, with every one of those pathetic knights that you sent to grovel at my feet. And of course every one of those knights was a painful reminder of one ill-judged action on his part. Can a man not be permitted to put his mistakes behind him?"

Parsifal looked curiously at Sir Kai, then at the woman, and his brow cleared. "Ah, now I understand," he said. "I didn't recognize you at first, but you are the lady whom Sir Kai slapped. And this is Sir Kai, isn't it?"

Lady Connoire continued her tirade. "That's right, and let me tell you something, O red knight, if you were thinking that sending those forty-one knights to me was going to make me fall into your arms when I saw you again, then you are

214

mightily mistaken! I never wanted your silly victims. I never liked having them at my feet, and I've never thought of you with anything but annoyance. I would no sooner fall in love with you than I would fall in love with my horse."

Sir Kai raised himself up on his good elbow and stared at Lady Connoire with astonishment.

"I am glad to hear it," Parsifal replied calmly. "Because, although you are very fair, I love only one woman – Queen Conduiramour. My wife."

"What?" Sir Kai and Lady Connoire said together.

"I never sought your favours, my lady," Parsifal said.

"Then why did you send all those knights to do honour to me?" Lady Connoire demanded.

Parsifal smiled without humour. "I hardly remember how it got started. Perhaps I did intend to punish Sir Kai for his unknightly behaviour. But for the past year, I have sent those knights to you simply because I wished to be rid of them, and sending them to you seemed as good as any other way. I see that I was mistaken, and I ask your forgiveness."

Sir Kai turned to King Arthur. "Help me to my feet, Arthur." The king did so. Sir Kai looked piercingly at Parsifal. "Then you're not in love with Connoire?"

"Is that her name?" Parsifal asked. "No. No, I'm not."

Sir Kai turned to Lady Connoire. "And you're not in love with him?" Lady Connoire, struck suddenly silent, shook her head. Sir Kai glowered at the crowd around them, then turned his fierce face back to Lady Connoire. "Well, then," he said. "I've something to say."

Lady Connoire raised her chin and met Sir Kai's gaze.

"I can't make flowery speeches," Sir Kai began, "and I wouldn't even if I could. I won't whimper at your feet like these callow puppies that call themselves knights these days, and I don't write poetry or play the damned rebec. I don't intend to change my manners or my way of life, but if you'll have me, Connoire, I'd be obliged if you'd marry me."

The incredulous silence that struck the watching crowd was so profound that Piers could hear the peep of a chickadee in the distant forest. Lady Connoire's expression did not change. Taking a deep breath, she said, "I don't like flowery speeches, and if you ever make one to me, I'll just laugh at you. I despise simpering poems, I hate the squealing of a rebec, and we'll see whether you'll change your manners or not. I'll marry you."

King Arthur, who was still supporting Sir Kai, said quietly, "I am not completely certain whether I have just witnessed a proposal or a challenge, but I wish you both very happy. Now I believe it would be best for Sir Kai to see my physician. Perhaps you knights could help him into the city. Yes, Lady Connoire, by all means go with him. The rest of us should retire to the banquet hall, where you may be sure we shall drink to you both. Come, Gawain. Come, Parsifal."

*

At the Christmas feast, Gawain was called on to tell the story of his quest, and Piers learned something about the nature of knightly stories. Gawain dwelt long on the details of the battle with Sir Malchance, and he told about his victory over the silly Sir Lejoie as if it were worthy of an epic. On the other hand, he passed very quickly over the grief-driven madness of the pathetic Sir Virgil, said nothing at all about Trevisant and his book, and spoke in only the vaguest terms about his trial in the Château Merveile. It came to Piers suddenly, in a flash of understanding, that the true story was not the story that most people wanted to hear. Gawain told the tale as it was expected and it became an enjoyable and easily forgettable story about battles of no particular importance.

Parsifal, on the other hand, was not so adept. When Gawain had finished his tale, and King Arthur asked Parsifal if he could tell about his own adventures, Parsifal rose slowly to his feet and said, "I've had no adventures. I have fought where I was threatened, but even a rat will do that. I earned the love of an incomparable woman, but I foolishly left her to look for glory. The only great deed I have ever had opportunity to do, I failed to achieve, and all my efforts to redeem myself for that failure have been useless."

Parsifal sat down again, and King Arthur rose.

"It has been well said, Parsifal. We have witnessed your knightly skill. Now we have witnessed your soul, and it is more knightly still. I stand ready to make you a knight, if you desire, and to declare you a fellow of my Round Table."

Parsifal replied slowly. "But I cannot stay at your court, your highness. Tomorrow I must go again on my search."

"You will do what you must," the king said. "But I would be honoured to have such a knight to join with me."

"If you wish it, sire," Parsifal said. And then, at King Arthur's direction, Parsifal knelt at the king's feet. The king touched Parsifal's shoulders lightly with his sword, then said, "Rise, Sir Parsifal, and welcome to the Fellowship of the Round Table. Be ever true to your God; protect always your neighbour; honour always your king."

11

THE GRAIL KING

Piers had no doubt that Parsifal would be departing the morning after the feast, so that evening he took his leave of Gawain. The knight looked mournful and said plaintively, "All my companions are deserting me for others," but when Piers hastened to explain, Gawain only laughed and flicked his cheek carelessly. "I'm joking. Go with God, lad."

Piers made his bed at the horse enclosure near Parsifal's mount. Sure enough, long before daylight Piers was awakened by a stirring in the pen, and there was Parsifal, saddling his horse. Piers rose at once. "Parsifal?"

"Pierre?"

"Piers," Piers corrected. "I've been waiting for you. I want to go along."

Parsifal hesitated. "I told you once that I want no page."

"I don't want to be a page anymore."

"Then what will you be?" Parsifal asked.

"Your companion?"

Again, there was a long pause. Then Parsifal said, "I would like a companion, I think."

Piers took a deep breath, tried to remember the elaborate speech he had been preparing ever since Parsifal had sent him away, but could not. He said, "I was wrong, Parsifal. I want to go with you until it is made right."

A bitter note crept into Parsifal's voice. "What if it is never made right? Are you ready to wander the rest of your life with me?"

"We'll find Munsalvaesche again. I know it. You'll have another chance to heal the fisherman king."

Parsifal turned back to his horse. "He's my uncle, you know," he said at last.

"I know. I read the hermit's book, too."

"All right," Parsifal said. "Get your horse."

Piers didn't move. "Before we go, I have something to give you." He reached into his saddlebag and produced the garland he had taken from the island. "It is a magic garland. It will bring you to the place that you seek."

Parsifal was still, and his shape in the darkness seemed to Piers to grow even darker. "I believe in no such magic," he said harshly. "There is no help for us in charms and make-believe."

Piers took a step closer. "Please."

"No!" Parsifal snapped.

"But why not try it?" Piers asked.

Parsifal glared at the garland for a moment. "You do not know how many times these past months I have thought I was close to my uncle's castle, only to have my hopes destroyed. I want no more false hopes. Take it out of my sight!"

Piers swallowed hard. "May I bring it with me? If I keep it in my pack?"

Parsifal frowned. "Do as you like. But don't show it to me again."

They rode side by side over the snowy fields, seldom speaking, looking neither to the right nor the left. As always, Parsifal set a gruelling pace. The sun rose, reached its zenith, then began to lower in the sky, and still they did not stop. Long after sundown, Parsifal reined in.

"We must eat," he muttered, as if grudging his body the time it required for food.

"You take off your armour and go hunting," Piers said. "I'll make camp."

Piers found a good campsite and collected dry wood for a fire. He cared for the horses, then examined Parsifal's armour. There were more dents and cuts in it than he could count. He tried to imagine how many blows it had taken to turn the magnificent red armour into the battered scrap that lay before him. He pounded out a few of the dents with a rock, but with no hammer, there was little he could do.

Parsifal returned with two hares, and they prepared them and ate in silence. After eating, Parsifal glanced at the armour beside Piers. "You're wasting your time," he commented. "It's hopeless."

"My father could fix it," Piers said.

"Your father?"

"He is a smith, the finest there is."

Parsifal looked curiously at Piers. "I've heard you speak of your mother, but never your father."

Piers poked at the fire but didn't reply.

So began Piers's second quest with Parsifal, but this one was very different. They rode side by side this time, but they seldom spoke. Parsifal did everything with a glowering intensity: he drove himself and his horse hard, he ate little and slept less, and the few times that he was challenged by other questing knights, he disposed of them quickly and impatiently. They found nothing that showed them the way to King Anfortas. It was bleak winter's travelling, but every night before he slept, Piers checked the Questing Garland in his pack, and each night he found the blooms still fresh. Though the garland could only work once he gave it to Parsifal, who had forbidden Piers to even mention it, its fragrance still gave Piers heart.

After perhaps two months, the weather warming somewhat but the trees still bare, they came to a dry wilderness. No brooks or rivers ran, and no puddles of melting snow muddied the paths. A faint, fetid smell hung in the air, as if something were decaying just over every hill. That night, for the first time that Piers could remember, Parsifal returned empty-handed from his hunt.

"It is a foul country," Parsifal said. He rolled up in his blankets, leaving Piers alone by the fire. Piers waited a moment to let Parsifal go to sleep, then crept to his pack and took out the Questing Garland. He gasped. The flowers, which had been fresh and fragrant only the night before, were wilting and were tinged with brown. The garland was dying.

He had dreamed of a time when Parsifal's

bitterness might subside and he would be able to give him the wreath, but now he realized he couldn't wait. Taking a deep breath, he walked over to Parsifal's prone form and gently laid the garland on Parsifal's feet. "I give it to you," Piers whispered.

Parsifal stirred. Opening his eyes, he gazed at Piers without expression. Then he looked at the garland. "I told you not to show me that again," he said. Sitting up, Parsifal crumpled the garland into a damp ball in his hands and threw it into the darkness.

Piers wept quietly that night, his tears streaking the dust on his face, until he slept. He awoke at dawn, feeling a warm breeze stir his blankets and listening to a strange and familiar sound. He rose quickly to investigate. "Parsifal!" he exclaimed. The knight rolled from his blankets, his hand on his sword. "Look!" Piers said.

A few yards away from the camp, just where Parsifal had thrown the garland, a fount bubbled and danced in the new light. A small stream had already formed and was flowing freely away to the east, toward the sun. The garland was gone.

Parsifal stared at the little fountain, but Piers began gathering their gear. "Come on, Parsifal!"

"Come where?" Parsifal asked, still gazing at the spring.

"To follow the water," Piers said. "We have to follow the water."

They rode beside the brook, which grew deeper and wider as they went, as if fed with underground springs. The breeze blew away the rotten smell, and the sun sparkled on the water. A fish jumped in the stream, and Piers's horse shied. As Piers leaned over to calm the animal, he caught a brief glimpse of something passing just under the surface of the water. It was there for moment, then gone, but Piers smiled. It was Ariel.

The stream became a wide, shallow river and then emptied into a broad lake that stretched as far as Piers could see. Without hesitation, he guided his horse into the lake and found that it was only a little more than a foot deep. "Come on, Parsifal!" he called over his shoulder. "Follow the water!" There was a moment of silence, then a splash as Parsifal plunged in beside him.

"Piers!" Parsifal demanded, riding up beside him. "Do you think this is from that garland?"

"Just follow the water."

"Tell me, Piers. I must know! Do you really believe that those flowers were magic?"

Piers glanced at Parsifal, whose face showed

doubt and confusion and anger. "I believe the person who told me they were," Piers said.

They rode on through the lake, the water never deeper than their horses' knees. "Someone coming," Parsifal said. Piers looked up. Still a mile distant was a figure on horseback, riding toward them through the lake. "A knight," Parsifal added.

The knight headed toward them, and a minute later they were face to face. The knight was as tall and powerful-looking as Parsifal, and his armour was of a brilliant crimson. He wore his helm with the visor down.

Parsifal spoke first. "Well met, friend," Parsifal said.

"Well met for one of us, but not for both," the knight replied. His voice had a familiar ring to it. "For I bring you a challenge."

"I don't want your challenge," Parsifal said.

"It is your destiny to fight me," the knight said simply.

Parsifal shrugged indifferently. "Who are you to tell me my destiny?"

"I am the knight you were born to fight. Do you refuse my challenge?"

Parsifal did not answer for a long time. He looked at the knight's armour, then looked at his own battered shell. "Yes, I refuse your challenge."

The knight laughed derisively. "Are you indeed the great Sir Parsifal? The knight whose feats are trumpeted across the land?"

"I am called Parsifal, yes."

"And yet a coward. Very well, then. Get down from that horse and kneel before me, you dog."

"And if I do not?"

"Then I shall draw my sword and beat you with it. And do not think that your armour will protect you, for I have slain more than one man who was fully armoured."

Parsifal's eyes flashed. Piers thought he was going to draw his sword and fight after all, but he did not. Instead, Parsifal's face grew prouder and fiercer than Piers had ever seen it, and he said in a ringing voice, "Go ahead, then. But you won't need to worry about my armour." And with that, Parsifal drew off his helm and threw it as far away as he could. The helm splashed in the marshy water, then sank.

"What are you doing?" the knight demanded.

Parsifal did not reply. He only pulled off his heavy gauntlets and threw them after his helm. Then he loosened his breastplate. "You wanted to beat me with your sword, friend. Have at it!" he shouted. He pulled his breastplate free and threw it disdainfully into the water between him and the knight.

Piers could only watch with horror as Parsifal deliberately removed every separate piece of his armour and threw each item into the lake. The knight was also too astonished to move. At last, Parsifal was down to his chain mail doublet and his sword. Wordlessly, Parsifal handed the sword to Piers, and then he removed the mail and threw it behind him. Where it sank, a fine mist of tiny bubbles rose to the surface.

"You're mad," the knight said.

"I told you! I don't want your challenge! I don't want to fight anymore! I don't care if you call me a coward, and I don't care what you say my destiny is! Go away!"

The knight reached up to his own helm, loosened it, then took it off. Piers gasped. The face that appeared before them was Parsifal's face, identical in every detail, except that the knight's skin was dark and his hair was white. A long scar on the knight's forehead was lighter than the rest of his face, which gave him a mottled look, almost as if he were striped. Now Piers realized why the knight's voice had sounded familiar. It was Parsifal's voice. "My name is Fierfils, and you cannot escape doing battle with me. It is your destiny to fight, and mine to defeat you. Draw your sword."

229

Parsifal reached out, and Piers gave him the sword, the perfectly balanced sword with the ornate letter T on the haft. Parsifal drew it from its scabbard and let the scabbard fall into the lake at his horse's feet. "You will have to achieve your destiny without me, brother," Parsifal said. And then he drew back his arm and threw his incomparable sword as far as he could. Its blade flashed twice as it spun through the air, and then it sliced into the water and disappeared.

Piers dragged his eyes away from the spot where the sword had fallen and turned back to Parsifal and Fierfils. The knight's face was blank with amazement. "But that sword was your dearest possession."

"Yes."

The water of the lake shivered, and fish began to jump all at once. A fresh wind blew a fine spray into Piers's face, and the surface of the lake behind Fierfils started to roil. "You fool!" Fierfils shrieked, and then the knight sank slowly from sight beneath the surface.

All was still. The waters grew calm, and the sun seemed to shine more brightly. Parsifal spoke softly. "You said that you read the hermit's book, didn't you, Piers?"

"Yes."

"Do you remember how King Anfortas got his wound?"

"Yes. He fought a knight who was like him in every way, but different." A delicious shiver crept up Piers's legs, then his back, and then tingled across his scalp. "I think we're almost there."

"Ride on," Parsifal said, and this time he took the lead.

They rode ten steps and Piers grew aware of a presence at his side. He looked down, and there was Ariel, smiling happily at him. She raised a finger to her lips, and Piers nodded. He glanced at Parsifal, to see if he had noticed, but Parsifal was too busy looking in the other direction, where Nimue walked sedately on his other side. Soon there were others – nymphs and water sprites and creatures Piers did not recognize – and they formed a solemn procession through the lake. The air before them shimmered, as if in the heat of midsummer, and then the castle Munsalvaesche was there, brilliant in the pale winter sun, its gate open wide.

Parsifal stopped his horse, looked at the castle, and wept. Dismounting, he knelt in the water and bowed his head. After a moment, he rose and continued on foot, tears still coursing down his cheeks. Piers dismounted as well, took Ariel's hand for a moment, then let it drop, and hurried after Parsifal. Parsifal stepped out of the water to the threshold of the gate. There, one of the ladies met him.

"Come in, sir knight," the lady said. "May I take you to your room?" Parsifal shook his head and walked past her.

Piers caught up to Parsifal, and together they crossed the great courtyard and entered the central keep. Parsifal did not hesitate, but walked directly back to the great banquet hall where they had dumbly witnessed the Grail procession. Dripping water and clad only in the stained linen shift that he had worn under his armour, Parsifal stepped into the splendid room.

King Anfortas was there, on the same dais where he had lain before, and his face was grey with pain. Parsifal crossed the banquet hall and stood before him. The king looked up, saw Parsifal, and said faintly, "Yes?"

Parsifal took the king's hand and knelt before him. "Dear Uncle," he said gently. "What ails you?"

It was the question. The question that King Anfortas had waited so long for the right person to ask. The question that Parsifal had not asked the last time. The question that would heal the king.

And the king was healed, immediately. Colour returned to his face, and he rose to his feet with a bound. "It is over!" he shouted. "Let the land be restored!"

Then the banquet hall was filled with joyous courtiers, shouting and singing and embracing each other. Parsifal stood silently in the midst of the dancing throng, and Piers stepped to one side to be out of the way. A tall figure loomed close, then took a position beside him. It was the man in motley who had mocked them from the castle wall. "I did not think you would return," he said.

"We have never stopped trying," Piers said. "Ever since that day that you taunted us."

The man smiled. "Then it worked." He bowed deeply and gracefully to Piers and disappeared in the crowd.

King Anfortas held up his hand for silence, and after several seconds managed to calm the celebrating courtiers. "But we are rude," he said. "We do not even know the name of the one who has delivered us." He turned to Parsifal.

Parsifal knelt before the king. "I am called Parsifal. I am the son of your sister Herzeloyde, and I am your servant."

King Anfortas stepped off the dais and raised Parsifal to his feet. "But no. I am yours. For as of this moment, you are the Grail King, Lord of the Schloss Munsalvaesche."

Parsifal shook his head. "No. I cannot be king here. My home is in the World of Men, and now that I have completed this task, I want only to return there, to my lady and my home."

King Anfortas did not seem disappointed. He nodded in acquiescence, then waved his hand. A woman entered the hall carrying a sword. The king said, "When you return there, you should have a sword."

Parsifal took the sword from the lady, and his eyes lit up. "But this is my own sword, that I threw away."

King Anfortas smiled. "That's right. As you have now learned, the things that you achieve by your own mighty deeds have no value until they are thrown away. But the things that are worth keeping – those things are yours for the asking. Before, this sword was a prize of war; now it is a gift. Take it. It was made for you, after all, by the greatest of all armourers, my servant and friend Trebuchet."

Parsifal looked fondly at the sword, then back at the king. "Trebuchet. He was one of the three who went away for your sake, wasn't he?"

"Yes. He and my sister Herzeloyde and my

brother Trevisant."

"They should be told that you are healed," Parsifal said thoughtfully. "When I return, I will do so. But there is one difficulty: I can find my mother and Trevisant, but I do not know where to seek this Trebuchet."

Piers stepped forward. "I think I know someone who does," he said.

12

THE SEEKERS

They set off three days later, renewed in every way. Parsifal wore a new, splendidly made suit of armour and Piers, a neatly cut suit of fine cloth. Parsifal's face had lost its bitter expression and now shone with relief, contentment, anticipation, and a hundred other pleasant emotions. As for Piers, he supposed that his face might be a bit radiant, too: Ariel and Nimue were riding with them.

Nimue had come to act as their guide, and she led them first to the forest home where Parsifal had been raised by his mother. Parsival planned to tell Lady Herzeloyde that her brother Anfortas had been healed, then bring her with him to Queen Conduiramour. "After all," he said with a rueful smile, "it was to bring my mother home that I left

Belrepeire to begin with."

"How long ago was that?" Piers asked. The passage of time was a bit fuzzy for him since his trip with Gawain to the Château Merveile.

"Almost a year," Parsifal replied, "for all it seems like a different lifetime."

Soon Parsifal began to recognize landmarks from his childhood, and then they arrived at his mother's home and found it empty. Piers did not even have to go inside to know that; a deserted house is unmistakable. What had once been a flower garden was now overgrown with weeds. A few sheep grazed in the yard, part of a larger flock that was on a nearby knoll. Parsifal stared at the cottage with dismay. "But where could she have gone?" he asked.

Dismounting, he disappeared into the house. Piers started to follow but Nimue caught his arm. "No, Piers."

Ten minutes later, Parsifal reappeared carrying some yellowed scraps of paper. "My father's letters," he said. "She used to read them every night. They've been chewed on by mice." The dismay in Parsifal's face was gradually being replaced by a calm and certain despair. "She must be dead," Parsifal said simply.

"Perhaps that shepherd may know something,"

Nimue suggested.

Among the sheep on the hill, a roughly clad man with a long staff was watching the travellers. Parsifal led his horse up the slope. "Good morrow, friend," he said. "Do you know the lady who lives in that cottage?"

"An't no lady there," the man said gruffly. He spat.

"No, not now," Parsifal said. "But there was a lady there at one time."

"Ay."

"Do you know what has become of her?"

"Nay, that be up to God now," the shepherd said.

Parsifal bowed his head. "Then she's dead. How did it happen?"

The man spat again and looked speculatively at Parsifal. "Never saw the sense in asking how. How don't matter to her, and if it don't matter to her, it an't none of my affair."

Parsifal frowned, and Nimue said gently, "The good man might be speaking wisdom. Must you know how she died?"

Parsifal nodded. "Yes."

The man shrugged. "The lady what lived there took to her bed and died, nobbut a week after her son went off to be a knight like her husband was. They do say the lady died of grief." Parsifal's face was still, and the shepherd added, "We buried her under that tree by the house."

They went back to the house and sat in silence while Parsifal knelt beside the slight mound under the tree. There was no marker. Parsifal absently pulled a few weeds, but it made no difference. In truth there was little else but weeds there. Parsifal stood. "But *I* came back, Mother. And I've brought you news. Your brother is well again. We are both well. Could you not have waited?"

Ariel slipped her hand into Piers's. Her eyes were wide and bright. Parsifal was silent for several minutes, as if expecting an answer, but none came, and at last he turned away and mounted his horse. They rode away.

Two days later, they trotted into the dusty yard of Trevisant's hermitage in the Gentle Wood. Terence was waiting for them, his horse saddled. "Well met, friends. Good day, my lady," Terence said, bowing to Nimue. "Trevisant told me they would be coming today, but he did not say you would be with them. I am glad to see you again."

"Hello, your grace," Nimue said. Piers wasn't sure how she did it, but Nimue somehow managed to convey a deep curtsey without getting out of her saddle.

Ariel stared at her mother. "Your grace?" she

whispered. "But this is the squire I was telling you about."

"Yes, my dear," Nimue said. "But he is also the Duke of Avalon, the son of the Enchanter, and one of the greatest princes of our world."

Piers gaped at the squire, who winked at him then stepped closer to Ariel and extended his hand. "But you must simply call me Terence. You, I suppose, are the one who followed us in the forest with a message for Piers."

"My daughter Ariel, your grace," said Nimue.

"Enchanted," Terence said, bowing again.

Parsifal watched all this patiently, but at this pause in the introductions said, "And where is Trevisant?"

Terence turned to Parsifal, his face serene. "By now, I imagine he is riding the hills of the Other World in armour again. But in this world he is no more. I buried him yesterday evening."

Parsifal closed his eyes. "We are too late again."

"You are Parsifal?" Terence asked. Parsifal nodded. "Have you come to tell Trevisant that the king has been healed?" Parsifal nodded again. "Then you are not too late. He knew. After all, it was his gift. He was very content the day he died."

"He was a good man," Parsifal said. "He tried to cure me of the bitterness of my soul."

Terence caught his horse's reins and swung into the saddle. "And did he?" he asked, interested.

"He helped," Parsifal said. He turned to Terence. "Shall we go, sir?"

Terence nodded, and they rode away. Piers noticed that Terence did not look back.

The miles seemed to fly by, and the horses never seemed to grow weary. By the third day after leaving Trevisant's home, they were riding through fields and farmlands that Piers recognized as belonging to Belrepeire. Although most of the fields lay dormant under the winter sun, they still showed signs of good husbandry. The travellers rode through the gate of Belrepeire just before noon.

A few servants, working in the courtyard, rose from their labour to look curiously at the cavalcade of visitors. An elderly man with a crisp stride and a firm chin stepped from the castle keep to meet them. Piers recognized Sir Reynold, Queen Connie's captain of the guards. "May I help you, friends?" he asked.

"Good morning, Reynold," Parsifal said. "I am glad to see you looking so well. Is your mistress at home?"

Sir Reynold looked sharply at Parsifal, then

rubbed his eyes. "By the sword of the king, it is you, isn't it? I do beg your pardon, my lord. My eyes... I'm afraid I'm not what I used to be."

"Nor am I," Parsifal replied. "Is Connie...?"

But Parsifal never finished his question, because at that moment the queen herself stepped out of the castle. She wore no ornaments and her dress was simple, but no one beholding her could doubt that this was a queen. Ariel clutched Piers's elbow, "Oh, Piers, she's beautiful."

Queen Connie looked at Parsifal, and her eyes glowed, but she did not step forward to greet him. "Welcome home, my lord," she said softly. Parsifal had begun to dismount, but at the queen's restrained tone, he hesitated. Conduiramour glanced once at the rest of the party, then looked back at Parsifal. "Have you done the great deeds you set out to do and become a knight?" she asked.

"I am a knight now, yes," Parsifal replied. His voice was steady, but his eyes were suddenly full of anxiety. "I am sorry that I have been gone so long, my queen."

"I suppose great deeds must take a long time," Queen Connie said. "Are these visitors people whom you met while doing great deeds?"

Parsifal blinked, then nodded. "Yes, except for Piers, here, of course."

The queen glanced at Piers, and her eyes widened. "Pierre? I am so sorry. I didn't recognize you at first. You are very different."

Suddenly tongue-tied and uncertain, Piers could only nod and glance anxiously at Parsifal. Piers had never imagined that Parsifal's homecoming might not be joyful. Then Nimue urged her horse forward and dismounted in front of the queen. "My lady, may I introduce myself? I am Nimue, but I am sometimes called the Lady of the Lake." Piers caught his breath. He hadn't realized that Nimue was the famous lady of his mother's stories. Conduiramour blinked as well, and Nimue continued, gesturing behind her. "This is my daughter, Ariel, and that is Terence, squire to Sir Gawain of Orkney. We ride with your husband as an escort. Indeed, he has done great deeds. He has saved a king and a kingdom, but when he was offered the throne of that great realm, he said that all he wanted to do was return to you."

Queen Connie swallowed, then turned her eyes again to Parsifal. Parsifal dismounted. "My love, I have been away too long. When I left you, I was full of foolish ideas about being a knight. I made a great mistake and caused a great harm. Since that time, I have been trying to remedy that harm. At last, with the help of Mistress Ariel and my friend Piers, I have done so."

Finding his tongue, Piers interjected, "Actually, the mistake was mostly my fault, anyway."

Neither Queen Connie nor Parsifal looked at him. Parsifal continued, "All the time I was gone, I never went an hour without longing for you. When I saw the pure white of the snow, I thought of your cheek. When I saw the red of a berry, I thought of your lips. When I heard the wind or the water or the song of the nightingale, I remembered your voice. I hated my quest because it kept me from your side, and I rejoiced when it was over only because it meant I could return to you."

A silence followed this speech as Conduiramour and Parsifal looked at each other. Ariel sighed deeply and squeezed Piers's hand.

And then Connie smiled and held out her hands, and Parsifal stepped forward and embraced her. "Then you are done with your questing?" she asked.

Parsifal released her and stepped back, still holding her at arms' length. "No," he said. "I have one more task to do." Connie's smile faded, and Parsifal said, "Will you come with me this time?" She smiled again, and then it was mostly more hugging and some kissing and even a few tears, and Parsifal was home.

Dinner that night was a joyous time. Queen Connie and the court of Belrepeire held an impromptu feast to celebrate Parsifal's return and to welcome their noble guests. Food was plentiful – Piers could not help contrasting such bounty with the starvation conditions that he and Parsifal had found here only a year before – and an air of warmth and contentment filled the hall. Conduiramour told her husband about the past year, filled with quiet triumphs, like the draining of a swamp to create a new field, and simple sorrows, like the peaceful death of the queen's old lady-in-waiting, Lisette. Parsifal listened to the voice of his love, and he rejoiced and mourned with her in her telling.

When she had done, Parsifal told Queen Connie the story of his quest. The tale was well worth hearing, full of mighty battles and courageous deeds, but Parsifal himself showed little interest in these. He dwelt much more on his time with the hermit Trevisant, who had taken him in, just when he had given up hope of ever achieving his quest, and on his regret that both Trevisant and his mother had died before he could see them again.

"Each of them gave me much," Parsifal said

reflectively. "My mother gave me life, and the hermit gave me hope."

"Perhaps that was what they were meant to do," Nimue said quietly. "They set off, so many years ago, to find the one who would break the spell and heal their brother. They didn't find him – they created him. Do not mourn these two; save your regrets for those whose lives serve no purpose at all."

Terence stretched lazily in his chair and sipped his wine. "There was a third who rode with Trevisant and Lady Herzeloyde, wasn't there?"

Parsifal nodded soberly. "Yes, the armourer Trebuchet. When Trevisant stopped searching and made his home in the Gentle Wood, this Trebuchet rode on alone." Parsifal turned to Queen Connie. "That is the last part of my quest. I must find this Trebuchet to tell him that his master is whole again."

"But how will you find him? Have you heard nothing of his whereabouts?" she asked.

Nimue sighed quietly. "That is the question, my lady. The good Trebuchet has not been heard from for more than twenty years. He has been much missed in the Other World, for there is no one who crafts such swords as he." She glanced at Terence. "As your master knows," she added.

Terence laughed lightly. "Oh? Is Gawain's sword Galatine the work of this armourer? Then he surely is a wizard. I know of none like it."

Parsifal turned to Piers. "I think Piers here knows where he is. Do you not?"

"I . . . I'm not sure," Piers said hesitantly. "But I think I know someone who can help us. My father." Piers felt Terence's eyes on him, and he blushed.

"Your father?" Parsifal asked.

Piers nodded. "Yes. He's a smith. I know that a smith is different from an armourer, but my father is . . . he knows how to . . . I'm not sure. But I just think he might know where this Trebuchet is," Piers finished lamely. He couldn't tell his friends all that he was thinking, because he wasn't sure what that was himself. But he remembered how his father had mentioned a faery armourer when he gave Trebuchet's sword to Sir Ither, and he remembered how he had seen the ornate "T" of Trebuchet on some of the arms and armour in his father's shop.

"Then it is decided," said Nimue. "Because the last charge that King Anfortas gave me before we left Munsalvaesche was to take you back to your parents."

*

247

They left the next morning, Nimue and Terence riding together in the lead, followed by Piers and Ariel, with Parsifal and Conduiramour trailing behind the others, lost in a year's supply of laughter and easy conversation. As before, time and distance seemed to melt around them, and before long Piers began to recognize landmarks. There was the path to the village where his mother did the marketing in her simple but elegant gowns; there was the bridge where he had fished; and there, just over the hill, was the wooded area behind which his parents lived.

Piers heard his father at work before he saw the house, a regular beating of steel on iron. A slow warmth began to fill Piers's breast, and he cocked his head to listen. Heavy beats – nothing very fine or delicate. Horseshoes, perhaps. Or a plough. Nimue glanced over her shoulder, then made way for Piers to take the lead.

With Ariel at his side, Piers rode through the trees and then into the dusty yard. Everything was as he remembered it: the small but neat house and the low, broad, solidly built shop – doors wide open to catch every cooling breeze. Piers reined in his horse, and sensed the others spreading out around him and stopping as well. And then the red glow that shone through the door of the shop was blocked by a formidable shadow, and Giles the Smith appeared at the door, followed by the slight, graceful form of Marie de Champagne. They were unchanged, as if Piers had been away for only a few minutes on an errand to the village. Piers found he could not speak, but could only smile with grateful contentment.

Giles frowned and glanced quickly at the row of mounted visitors. He started to speak, then stopped as his gaze fell on Parsifal. He stepped closer. "Whence came thee by that armour, Sir Knight?" he demanded abruptly.

Parsifal met the smith's gaze squarely. "It was given me," he replied simply. "How else could such armour be gained?"

Giles could not tear his eyes from the armour. "Ay," he muttered. "How else indeed? But who gave it?"

Parsifal hesitated. "Know you this armour, friend?" Giles nodded slowly, and Parsifal began to smile. He dismounted and drew his sword from its scabbard. "And know you this sword?"

Giles looked at the sword, the same sword that he had given Sir Ither on the day when Piers had left home, and then the smith's hard, craggy face twisted. Tears began to flow down his cheeks, and he dropped to his knees before Parsifal. "Tell me, sir, I beg you. Let me not wait another moment. Is it well with my master?"

Parsifal nodded. "King Anfortas is well."

Giles bowed his head, and his body relaxed. Piers dismounted and walked slowly toward his father. "Then it's true," he said softly. "I hardly dared to think it, but it's true. You are Trebuchet, aren't you, father?"

The smith raised his head and stared, uncomprehending, at Piers, but before he could speak, Piers's mother gasped. *"Mordieu! Mais ce courtisan gallant. . . . C'est mon Pierre!"*

Piers smiled at her and said, "Hello, mother," but turned back to his father. Reaching out, he took his father's hand and raised him to his feet. "I've come home, father."

"Piers," the smith said softly. "I wouldn't have recognized you. You've grown a span, I believe, and where did all this muscle come from?" His eyes dwelt for a moment on Piers's arms.

Piers grinned. "Not from eating regular meals, I can tell you that." And then he reached out and clasped his father, and then his mother joined their embrace, and they were all crying.

When at last they had separated, Piers remembered the others. "Father, mother, let me introduce you to my friends. Father, this is

Parsifal, the one you went away to search for. He healed King Anfortas."

Giles – or, rather, Trebuchet – looked intently at Parsifal. "Thank you," he said gruffly. His dark brow furrowed slightly as he gazed at the knight's face. "But do I know you?"

Parsifal shook his head. "No, but you knew my mother. Lady Herzeloyde."

Trebuchet took a deep breath, then beamed with delight. Piers hurried on. "And with Parsifal is his wife, Queen Conduiramour, and this is Nimue." Piers paused. "Mother, when you used to tell me stories about her, you called her the Lady of the Lake. And this is Terence, squire to Sir Gawain." Piers's mother gaped at them both, as if figures from a dream had come to life before her. "And finally," Piers said, "this is my good friend Ariel."

Piers's mother managed to shake off her paralysis and drop a deep curtsey to the company. Trebuchet bowed to Nimue. "Good day, my lady. Forgive me for not recognizing you, either. It has been many years."

"And you have always noticed a good suit of armour before you had eyes for people anyway, haven't you?" Nimue said, a dimple showing.

Trebuchet glanced at Parsifal's armour. "It is only that . . . well, I made that suit."

Nimue chuckled. "We have come to bring you tidings. King Anfortas is healed, and Munsalvaesche has been delivered. Your quest in the World of Men is complete. The king has asked me to invite you to return to your place there."

Piers's mother was very still, her eyes on the dust, but Piers's father stepped back beside her and put one heavy arm around her shoulders. "I am glad that my master has been healed. I have prayed for him nightly. But I cannot return. My home is here now, with the wife I love."

"Why, that is my case exactly," interjected Parsifal. "I am weary of questing, and I wish to remain with my lady, Conduiramour. Perhaps, since we share the same dream, we might share the same home. Our castle of Belrepeire could use an armourer and smith."

Queen Connie, who had been looking with interest at Piers's mother, said, "And I am very much in need of a lady-in-waiting. My own beloved dresser Lisette has only recently died. My lady, forgive me, but I have never seen a dress like yours, cut in such a marvellous style."

Marie de Champagne's eyes lit with a sudden fire. "It is my own design, my lady. It would look better with finer cloth."

"You shall have it," Queen Connie said.

Piers's mother turned beseeching eyes toward her husband, but the armourer was already nodding. "Ay," he said. "'Tis time." Then Trebuchet looked again at Piers. "And you shall live in a castle, as you always wanted, and you can become a squire and courtier."

Piers shook his head, his eyes gleaming. "I'd rather not, thank you. But do you think you could teach me to make nails?"

AUTHOR'S NOTE

When the legends about King Arthur and his knights of the Round Table were first written down, there were no spelling rules. There were no dictionaries, no helpful rhymes about "i" before "e" and no weekly spelling quizzes. No one ever had to ask "Does spelling count?" because it didn't. As a result, different writers spelled words differently, depending on their taste, their country of origin, and sometimes, I suspect, according to their mood. This state of affairs wasn't all bad, of course (see "no weekly spelling quizzes" above), but it could be confusing.

The confusion seems particularly noticeable when it comes to names. The name of King Arthur's great knight Gawain, for instance, is also spelled Gawaine, Gawan, and (by the Welsh) Gwalchmai. (The Welsh tend to be independent-minded; for instance, their spelling of the name Merlin is "Myrddin.")

The story that I have retold in this book is an ancient one, but the first written form of it that we know is by a French poet named Chrétien de Troie, and he called his hero Perceval. Chrétien never finished his story, though, and so other writers took it up and wrote their own endings – each in his own language, using his own spelling. The hero became Percival, Parzival, Parsifal, and (to the Welsh again)

Peredur. In my own retelling, I have followed the version of the story that was written in 1415 by a German knight and singer of tales named Wolfram von Eschenbach, but like earlier storytellers, I have spelled the names however I wanted. Thus Wolfram's Condwiramurs became Conduiramour; Meljahnz became Malchance; Antikonie became Antigone; Vergulaht became Virgil; and Parzival became Parsifal. I just liked those spellings better.

No matter how his name's spelled, there is no knight whose story has been told more often than Parsifal's. His story has been the basis of countless tales, songs, operas, movies, and at least one silly and self-important psychology book. Something about a wild man of the woods who wants to become a knight catches our fancy. Something about a quest for a miraculous, life-giving object (the Grail) speaks to people in all ages. There's even something deep and meaningful about how Parsifal achieves his quest – not by doing great deeds, but by asking one simple question. I don't pretend to understand why these things are so powerful – because I try very hard not to sound like a silly and self-important psychologist – but whatever it is, people love this story.

At any rate, I do.

G.M.

THE SQUIRE'S TALES

Read more of *The Squire's Tales!*

SQUIRE TERENCE AND THE MAIDEN'S KNIGHT

When Terence, a young orphan, meets a
stranger called Gawain, he embarks on
the adventure of a lifetime.

ISBN 0 7534 1032 X

THE SQUIRE, HIS KNIGHT AND HIS LADY

Squire Terence and Sir Gawain are off
questing again, but this time there's a chance
that Gawain won't come back . . .

ISBN 0 7534 1031 1

THE SAVAGE DAMSEL AND THE DWARF

When an evil knight besieges Lady Lynet's castle,
she sets out to recruit a rescuer, but a scruffy
serving boy isn't who she has in mind!

ISBN 0 7534 1048 6